FIRST THING WE DO, LET'S DEREGULATE ALL THE LAWYERS

FIRST THING WE DO, LET'S DEREGULATE ALL THE LAWYERS

CLIFFORD WINSTON
ROBERT W. CRANDALL
VIKRAM MAHESHRI

BROOKINGS INSTITUTION PRESS
Washington, D.C.

Copyright © 2011
THE BROOKINGS INSTITUTION
1775 Massachusetts Avenue, N.W., Washington, DC 20036.
www.brookings.edu

Library of Congress Cataloging-in-Publication data
Winston, Clifford, 1952–
  The first thing we do, let's deregulate all the lawyers / Clifford Winston,
Robert W. Crandall, and Vikram Maheshri.
    p.   cm.
  Includes bibliographical references and index.
  ISBN 978-0-8157-2190-1 (pbk. : alk. paper)
  1. Legal ethics—United States. 2. Lawyers—United States. 3. Legal ethics—
Economic aspects—United States. I. Crandall, Robert W. II. Maheshri, Vikram.
III. Title.
  KF306.W48 2011
  174'.30973—dc23   2011022124

9 8 7 6 5 4 3 2 1

Printed on acid-free paper

Typeset in Sabon

Composition by Oakland Street Publishing
Arlington, Virginia

Printed by R. R. Donnelley
Harrisonburg, Virginia

15539985

mh

Contents

Acknowledgments   vii

1 Introduction   1

2 The Market for Lawyers   9

3 Evidence of Earnings Premiums in the Legal Profession   24

4 Sources of Lawyers' Earnings Premiums   57

5 Welfare Costs   73

6 The Case for Deregulating Entry into the Legal Profession   82

7 Toward Policy Reform   95

References   100

Index   107

Acknowledgments

We are especially grateful to Jesse Gurman for his contributions and valuable insights on the issues raised in this book. We also acknowledge important contributions made by David Burk, Kyungmin Kim, and Adriane Fresh. We received useful comments on specific chapters from Ian Ayres, Gary Burtless, William Dickens, Jay Ezrielev, Richard Geddes, William Henderson, Jeffrey Kling, Ashley Langer, George Leef, Robert Litan, J. J. Prescott, Mark Ramseyer, Tara Watson, and seminar participants at Cornell, George Mason, and Oxford Universities. Finally, we are grateful to the referees and Ted Gayer for their very helpful comments and to Martha Gottron for her usual superb editorial work.

CHAPTER ONE

Introduction

In late 2000 Justin Anthony Wyrick Jr. became the most requested legal expert on the website AskMeHelpDesk.com. To the great surprise of many bloggers and their followers, "Justin" was actually a fifteen-year-old high school student named Markus Arnold who apparently had never read a law book. The American Bar Association (ABA) was not impressed. In its view, Arnold had committed a serious ethical violation by misrepresenting himself as a lawyer.

Arnold was never prosecuted, but in an earlier episode Rosemary Furman nearly went to prison for trying to help people solve their legal problems without having a license to practice law. As recounted by Leef (1998), Furman was a legal secretary in Florida who decided to go into business for herself in 1972 by preparing and filing the necessary legal papers for people seeking a divorce. Her customers sought out her services and willingly paid for them; no one ever complained about her work. Despite this problem-free track record, the Florida Supreme Court in 1984 ordered her jailed for practicing law without a license. As it turned out, Furman never served any jail time, but only because Governor Bob Graham intervened.

Lawyers are among the 20 percent of the U.S. labor force that is required to obtain a government license to practice a profession (Kleiner 2006)—a requirement that may not be justified, as suggested by the preceding anecdotes, because some legal services could be competently provided by persons who have not had a formal legal education and who have not passed a state bar examination to obtain a license. Even people who do have a legal education are prevented from taking a bar examination and practicing law in all but a few states unless they graduated from an ABA-accredited law school. And ABA regulations prevent licensed lawyers who work for firms that are not owned and managed by lawyers from providing legal services to parties outside their firm. The ABA-imposed entry barriers are one important factor that we argue unnecessarily raises the cost of legal services. Before discussing the other important factor—that lawyers have become an effective interest group—we summarize how the ABA came to exert such a powerful influence on the practice of law.

The Evolution of the ABA's Influence

The association first attempted to include its accreditation of law schools as part of states' occupational licensing of lawyers in 1921, when, claiming concern over the quality of the legal education being administered, it adopted a statement of minimum standards of legal education and instituted a policy of publishing a list of law schools that complied with those standards. Whether this policy had beneficial effects and was justified is unclear: it is difficult not only to measure the quality of the legal education at the time but to verify that the ABA's accreditation standards improved it. Some commentators argue that the true motivation for the standards was to prevent minorities and the poor from joining the profession (Auerbach 1971). If true, that motivation would undermine an alleged benefit of occupational licensing: that it can increase the presence of minority workers by serving as an imprimatur of worker quality.[1]

1. Law and Marks (2009) test the effects of occupational licensing laws on minorities and find that they helped minorities in some occupations, but they do not report results for lawyers in their study. Lehmann (2010) finds that, compared with whites of similar credentials, blacks are much more likely to be hired by the best law firms. But they are assigned to worse tasks and less likely to be made partner because they are given less desirable work at the beginning of their careers.

Initially, state legislatures were not persuaded by the ABA's alleged justification for its standards, and four years after the standards were developed, not a single state required graduation from an ABA-accredited law school for admission to the bar. But by the 1950s the U.S. Department of Health, Education, and Welfare had recognized the Council of the ABA Section of Legal Education and Admissions to the Bar as the sole accrediting agency for degree-granting law schools, and about half the states had education requirements based on ABA standards. Friedman (1962, p. 153) suggested that the other states did not have such requirements because many state legislators themselves were graduates of unaccredited schools: "If they voted to restrict admission to the profession to graduates of approved schools, in effect they would be voting that they themselves were not qualified." Friedman later predicted that as more legislators were trained at accredited law schools, the ABA standards would be more broadly accepted (Fossum 1978). Indeed, Friedman's forecast has proved to be correct: today, all but a few states, notably California, require would-be lawyers to have graduated from an ABA-accredited law school, and every state except Wisconsin requires them to pass a bar exam.[2]

State governments also allow the ABA to enact regulations that govern the type of legal services that firms and individuals can offer. A firm is prohibited from offering legal services unless it is owned and managed by lawyers. The ABA defines the practice of law to prevent nonlawyers from providing what it deems to be legal products and services. Not surprisingly, its definition of the practice of law is expansive and includes nearly every conceivable legal service. The ABA has urged states to invigorate enforcement of practice restrictions on non-lawyers (Hadfield 2008a), even to restrict the sale of simple, standard-form wills as the unauthorized practice of law.

---

2. Wisconsin allows graduates of the University of Wisconsin Law School to practice law without passing a bar examination.

Lawyers as an Interest Group

With the help of the ABA, lawyers have developed into a powerful interest group that limits its membership. Unlike most other interest groups, lawyers benefit from government policies that increase the demand for their services.

The symbiotic relationship between policymakers and the legal profession has roots that can be traced to the formative years of the United States. In an 1816 letter to Benjamin Austin, Thomas Jefferson lamented that lawyers "by their numbers in the public councils, have wrested from the public hand the direction of the pruning knife."[3] Shepard (1981) documents the concern that lawyers may have been overrepresented in powerful state government positions during the nineteenth century, when, for instance, lawyers constituted 34 percent of the 1850 Virginia legislature despite making up less than 1 percent of the largely agrarian population. Between the Civil War and the 1950s, lawyers won approximately half of all gubernatorial elections (Schlesinger 1957).

With the rapid growth of the federal government following the New Deal, federal legislative positions became substantially more powerful than their counterparts at the state level. During the past forty years, nearly 60 percent of the members of the U.S. Senate and 40 percent of the members of the U.S. House of Representatives held a JD (juris doctor).[4] In the same period, four of the eight presidents also studied and practiced law before embarking on their political careers. Generally, an interest group can more easily gain from the political process when it "speaks the same language" as the public officials whose policies it is trying to influence. Accordingly, it is not

3. The quote comes from *The Writings of Thomas Jefferson*, edited by H. A. Washington (New York: H. W. Derby Publishers, 1861).

4. The 91st Congress (1969–70) contained 58 senators and 219 representatives with a law degree. Lawyers' grip on legislative power has persisted; the 111th Congress (2009–10) contains 57 senators and 168 representatives with a JD. Those figures are taken from the Congressional Research Service's periodic publication "Membership of the Congress: A Profile."

surprising that members of the legal profession benefit when lawyers lobby former practitioners.

Basic economics suggests that entry barriers to the legal profession, regulations on the type of legal services that firms and individuals can provide, and government-induced demand for lawyers will raise the price of legal services. In this book, we argue that this higher price cannot be justified as the "cost" of ensuring that uninformed consumers of legal services are served by competent lawyers and that socially desirable policies are implemented and executed. Instead, the forces that reduce the supply of and increase the demand for lawyers create significant social costs including a sizable deadweight loss from higher legal fees, less innovation by law firms and lawyers, a misallocation of the nation's labor resources, and socially perverse incentives for attorneys in their collective behavior as an interest group to support inefficient regulatory, liability, patent, and other policies that preserve and enhance their wealth.

To address those costs and improve social welfare, we argue that deregulating entry by individuals and firms into the legal profession is desirable to force lawyers to compete more intensely with each other and to face competition from nonlawyers and firms that are not owned and managed by lawyers. Occupational licensing may be justified to protect consumers if they have imperfect information about the quality of a service being offered, but the theoretical and empirical evidence supporting occupational licensing for lawyers is weak. We do not oppose lawyers continuing to acquire credentials to signal their competence and quality, but allowing the ABA to enjoy a monopoly on law school accreditation and the states to require that lawyers pass a licensing exam is not necessary to facilitate informed decisions by consumers of legal services.

Characterizing the Empirical Debate

An overview of the empirical debate is provided in figure 1-1, where w_0 denotes lawyers' wages without the effects of occupational licensing and entry restrictions on supply, S_0, and of government policies on

Figure 1-1. *The Market for Lawyers*

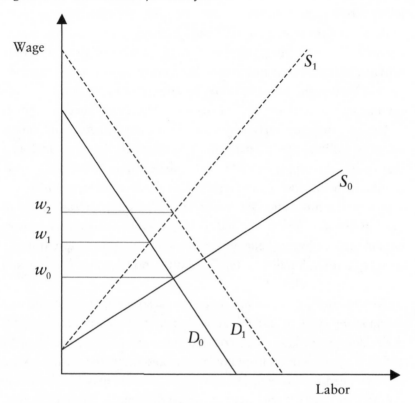

Source: Authors.
Note: See text for explanation of terms.

demand, D_0. Occupational licensing and entry restrictions cause the supply of lawyers to shift inward and become more inelastic, as indicated by S_1, which causes lawyers' wages to rise to w_1. Public policies that induce firms and individuals to hire lawyers shift the demand for lawyers to D_1, causing lawyers' wages to rise even more to w_2. Our interest is in whether the increase in lawyers' wages caused by entry restrictions and government-induced demand for lawyers is unjustified on efficiency grounds or, alternatively, is justified because of lawyers' unobserved skills and abilities and their working environment, because consumers receive higher quality legal services than they would receive without occupational licensing, and because lawyers contribute to implementing and executing beneficial public policies.

As regulatory economists, we find it natural to reason that occupational licensing, like other regulations that restrict entry, benefits existing suppliers by limiting competition. Thus its primary effect is to generate earnings premiums to practitioners in a particular profession such as law—earnings premiums that could be inefficient.

Labor economists are cautious about reaching the conclusion that workers in a particular profession such as law receive inefficient earnings premiums, noting the possibility that empirical estimates of wage premiums actually capture returns to unobserved skills, abilities, and working conditions, and that such returns are justified on efficiency grounds.[5] If this possibility is true, lawyers may receive earnings premiums that are unrelated to market inefficiencies caused by restrictions on entry and competition and that thus do not reflect social costs. We recognize this concern and therefore conduct a battery of tests to examine whether our estimates of earnings premiums can be explained by unobserved factors that reflect efficiencies, but we find no evidence that such efficiencies contribute to explaining lawyers' premiums.

Hadfield (2008b) summarizes the law literature that criticizes lawyers for being self-interested at the expense of consumers of legal services and the ABA for initiating regulations, including unauthorized-practice-of-law restrictions, which promote the interests of lawyers. This literature focuses on the costs to lawyers' reputations and to consumers who do not have access to legal services, but it does not discuss our concern about lawyers' potentially counterproductive role in maintaining inefficient public policies and how those policies benefit lawyers. If the demand for lawyers is increased by government policies that raise social welfare, then those benefits should be balanced against increases in lawyers' earnings. But we find that the policies that increase lawyers' earnings premiums have been assessed

---

5. Unobserved differences in skills refer to differences in skills among lawyers that we as empirical analysts are unable to observe. This does *not* imply that those differences in lawyers' skills are not observed by consumers of legal services.

empirically by scholars and found to have produced little improvement in economic welfare and are likely to have reduced it.

In this book, we recommend the deregulation of the legal profession, a recommendation that is justified even if entry restrictions do not generate inefficient earnings premiums. If lawyers' wages reflect only observed and unobserved differences in skills and ability, then consumers of legal services would continue to recognize those differences in the absence of occupational licensing requirements. Deregulation would also be justified even if the policies that increase lawyers' earnings premiums generate significant social benefits because lawyers would still be hired to implement those policies in a more competitive environment.

Finally, we do not minimize the vital role that lawyers in the United States play in supporting democratic institutions, protecting individual rights, and the like. But lawyers can also be judged on their effectiveness in contributing to economic activity and efficiency both within and outside their profession. We conclude that lawyers' performance on that score would improve greatly in a more competitive environment for legal services.

CHAPTER TWO

The Market for Lawyers

According to the Current Population Survey, approximately one million lawyers are currently working in the United States in law firms, government offices, and the legal departments of private corporations. This figure may comport with the conventional view that the United States has too many lawyers, but occupational licensing requirements have in fact constrained the supply of lawyers. In this chapter we provide an overview of the various policies that have affected the supply of and demand for lawyers and then estimate lawyers' aggregate annual earnings.

The Role of Law Schools in Limiting the Supply of Lawyers

As noted, to obtain a license to practice law, an individual must typically gain admission to a law school accredited by the American Bar Association and pass a state bar examination. The ABA's rigorous accreditation process takes a minimum of four years, including, for new law schools, an initial year during which the school must have been in operation before the ABA accreditation process can begin. The ABA has yet to consider online or foreign law schools for accreditation.[1]

1. The ABA has put off a decision on whether to accredit foreign law schools by saying it wishes to study the matter more fully. In June 2008 the Peking University of Transnational Law announced its intention to seek accreditation from

Figure 2-1. *Number of ABA-Approved Law Schools, 1923–2006*

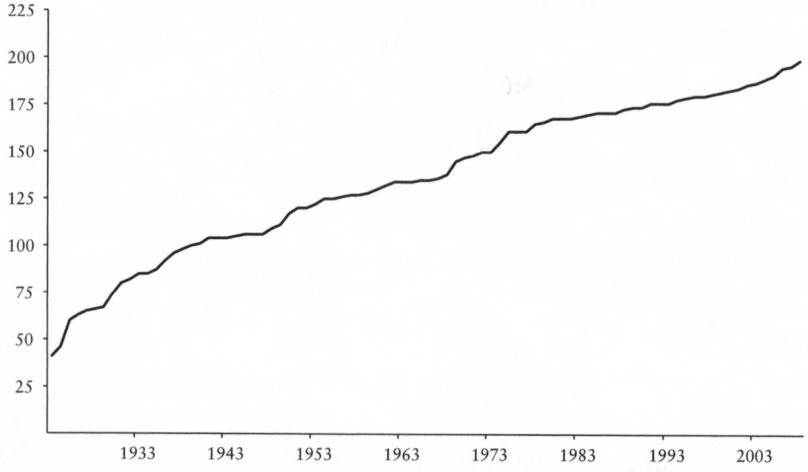

Source: American Bar Association.

Figure 2-1 shows the growth in the number of law schools approved by the ABA to grant law degrees since it began accrediting schools during the 1920s. The growth in accredited schools has slowed in the past three decades—the ABA has accredited only about thirty new law schools since 1979 (and rejected the accreditation of an unknown number of other schools; the ABA does not disclose a list of schools it has been unwilling to accredit). The ABA has even put some accredited law schools, such as Golden Gate University and Whittier College, on probation because their students' first-time bar passage rate was too low, and it has refused to renew some other law schools' accreditation until those schools have satisfied certain conditions.

The ABA's actions may be justified as maintaining and signaling the quality of legal education in the United States. But the ABA has refused to provide further information about a law school's quality beyond its accreditation status and has continually issued disclaimers

the ABA, so its graduates could potentially practice law in the United States. But the ABA said it would not consider the accreditation of any particular foreign law school until it completed its broader assessment.

of any law school rating system.[2] This policy is hardly consistent with the view that the ABA wants prospective law students and employers to be more informed about a law school's quality. As of 2010, 200 institutions in the United States were ABA-approved to confer law degrees, 7 of which had received only provisional accreditation. A few states, including California, have their own accreditation process and allow students who do not graduate from an ABA-accredited law school to sit for their bar examinations.[3]

Law school applicants are generally required to take the Law School Admissions Test (LSAT) and to report their scores. Thus, the number of distinct individuals who take the LSAT in any given year is a reasonable lower bound on the number of people in the United States interested in entering the legal profession. According to data from the Law School Admission Council, the number of unique first-time LSAT test takers has averaged nearly 100,000 a year from 1997 through 2004.[4] Only a very small percentage of people who take the test are discouraged from eventually applying to law school (although the expense and opportunity cost of three years in law school may discourage many from taking the test in the first place). The total number of law school applicants admitted to at least one law school averaged 53,300 a year during 1997–2004; thus, roughly half of the 800,000 law school applicants during the period were not admitted anywhere.[5] The Law School Admission Council has reported that the

2. The ABA recently passed Resolution 10A to "examine any efforts to publish national, state, territorial, and local rankings of law firms and law schools."

3. California's bar exam is considered to be among the most difficult in the country to pass, and it effectively serves as a screening device to limit the number of practicing attorneys in the state.

4. The Law School Admission Council is a nonprofit corporation that seeks to ease the admission process for law schools and their applicants. The council is best known for administering the Law School Admission Test.

5. John Nussbaumer, "The Door to Law School," Presentation at the University of Massachusetts School of Law, October 2010, presents data indicating that 60 percent of African American law school applicants from Fall 2000 to Fall 2009 did not receive an offer of admission from any law school. The "shut-out" rate was 45 percent for Hispanic applicants and 31 percent for Caucasian applicants.

recession, which began in late 2007, appears to have initially induced more people to pursue a career in law, as evidenced by an increase in LSAT test taking.[6]

Given that 95 percent of people who enroll in an ABA-accredited law school eventually pass a state bar examination, the primary factor that limits the supply of lawyers in the United States is clearly the number of available spaces in those schools. Indeed, the number of applicants to U.S. law schools has risen more than 50 percent since 1976, while total enrollments have increased only 26 percent. As noted, an unknown number of individuals may be discouraged from even applying to law school because they are unwilling to incur the opportunity cost and expense of a three-year course of study that can cost upward of $150,000 at some premier institutions.[7]

Existing and new law schools could provide capacity for additional law students, which could possibly reduce average costs and therefore tuition expenses and other fees to students. But existing law schools do not appear to have a significant interest in expanding their class sizes. Many law schools want to maintain a reputation for having strong students and fiercely competitive admissions. Sauder and Espeland (2007) confirm widely held beliefs that *U.S. News & World Report* rankings—which place large weights on the grade point average and LSAT scores of incoming students—strongly influence how the nation's law schools are managed and allocate resources.[8] Any law school that is not particularly concerned with its academic reputation and wishes to expand its class size is constrained by the risk of being

6. Debra Cassens Weiss, "LSAT Test-Takers Jump by Nearly 20%; Should They Consider the Alternatives?" *ABA Journal*, November 23, 2009. By 2011 the recession had taken its toll, with the number of law school applicants down 10 percent from 2010.

7. A November 2009 University of California Regents report to the state Assembly Committee on Finance indicated that prospective total annual fees could rise from $35,000 in 2009 to $50,000 in 2012 for California residents attending law schools at University of California campuses.

8. Martha Neil, "ABA Group: US News Law School Rankings 'Not Entirely Benign,' but We're Stuck with Them," *ABA Journal*, July 27, 2010, discusses a July 2010 ABA report that identifies how the *US News* rankings influence law schools' operating policies and adversely affect students.

put on probation by the American Bar Association because it has accepted too many students who fail to pass the bar. We take issue later with the requirement that an individual must pass a bar examination to practice law.

Law schools that want to expand class sizes significantly would also have to hire additional faculty and expand office space. Many law schools have taken those steps in the past thirty years, as indicated by a decline in the average student-to-faculty ratio of 29-to-1 in 1978 to 15-to-1 in 2008.[9] But the U.S. Government Accountability Office (2009) alleges those actions are motivated by competition among schools to rise in the *U.S. News* rankings, which also place significant weight on student-faculty ratios, and have led to only a limited expansion in enrollments and thus to sharp increases in tuition. Macchiarola and Macchiarola (2010) argue that the GAO's conclusion is misplaced and point out that tuition increases would be curbed if not for the ABA's accreditation process, which shields law schools from low-cost competition such as online law programs, certain accelerated two-year curricula, and apprenticeships.

The largest share of additional spaces for law students is therefore likely to come from new law schools. However, the creation of such schools responds very slowly to growing student demand because new law schools must first successfully complete the ABA's multiyear accreditation process if their graduates are to be able to take the bar examination in most states.

In sum, both existing and new law schools have gradually enabled more students to enroll, but this growth has been far outpaced by the demand for law degrees from ABA-accredited institutions. The constraints on the growth in the capacity of both types of law schools may have therefore prevented the supply of lawyers from increasing sufficiently to bid down any potential earnings premiums that derive from practicing law. In addition, the ABA has attempted to discourage individuals from attending non-ABA-accredited law schools by urging states that require a degree from an accredited law school as a condi-

9. "Law School Faculties 40% Larger than 10 Years Ago," *The National Jurist*, March 9, 2010.

tion of practicing law to charge legal practitioners without such a degree with the unauthorized practice of law by nonlawyers.

Government-Induced Demand for Lawyers

Even as the supply of lawyers has been constrained by the ABA and state licensing laws, the *demand* for lawyers in the public and private sector has experienced continual growth, thanks in part to government policies that require private firms to retain legal counsel or encourage them to engage in litigation. With the supply of lawyers restricted, increases in demand are raising wages and generating significant occupational earnings premiums. Moreover, as we argue later, the policies that have increased those premiums have questionable social benefits, and it is even more questionable whether the benefits they do generate exceed the policies' costs, including the expenditures on lawyers.

Because lawyers in the public sector (and usually in the private sector) are involved in nearly all government policies, we focus on a subset of the most important and contentious policy areas that help generate greater demand for attorneys and their services. For example, environmental standards governing pollution emissions and discharges are determined by competing teams of lawyers in the relevant administrative agencies—the Environmental Protection Agency or its state-level equivalents—and by additional lawyers employed by industrial firms, utilities, trade associations, distributors, and nonprofit interest groups. Proceedings to establish final rules may take several years, and even after a rule is established, a party may sue the administrative agency, resulting in lengthy judicial review and sometimes a repetition of the entire process.

Lawyers are also central to the resolution of intellectual property disputes. In some states, rules imposed by state bar associations require individuals engaged in Patent Office disputes to be represented by an attorney.[10] Jaffe and Lerner (2004) point out that the number of patents and patent lawsuits has more than doubled since a new U.S.

---

10. In *Sperry* v. *State Bar of Florida*, the Supreme Court ruled in 1963 against the Florida State Bar Association's rule.

Court of Appeals was established in 1982 to adjudicate intellectual property disputes. As a result, lawyers are routinely called upon to write patent applications because applicant companies know that most patents' validity will eventually be determined in a federal court.

Still another example of government-induced demand for legal services is the growth in the past few decades of liability suits, particularly class-action suits, in response to a product defect, accident, or financial reversal. In the United States private individuals and the government may bring liability suits; the most well-known litigation in the past few decades has involved the adverse effects of tobacco and asbestos on exposed individuals' health.

In class-action liability suits, lawyers represent a large number of individuals who are essentially bystanders in the process. Those lawyers obtain a jury trial and are generally paid on a contingency-fee basis. Because the cost of defending this type of suit may be high, and the cost of losing one even higher, large firms or other defendants with deep pockets are often induced to pay the plaintiffs to settle before trial. Most of those suits are litigated under state laws. Some state governments, such as Texas, have initiated tort reforms, but legal institutions in most jurisdictions still appear to promote litigation—or the threat of litigation—and, as a result, excessive attention to the reduction of risk. According to the professional services firm Towers Perrin, in 2003 the cost of the tort system as a share of GDP was 2.2 percent in the United States but only 0.7 percent in the United Kingdom and France, where class-action suits are rare.[11]

State laws have also increased the demand for lawyers. For example, since the 1960s states have enacted consumer protection acts (CPAs), which were intended to increase the resources available to pursue consumer protection cases; however, in practice, the acts have greatly

11. The Class Action Fairness Act of 2005 was intended to reduce "forum shopping" in tort case filings by shifting many of them to the federal courts. It is not clear whether the act has notably reduced the costs of the liability system. The European Union has recently begun to consider new forms of legal redress for consumers. See European Commission, *Green Paper on Consumer Collective Redress*, November 2008 (http://ec.europa.eu/consumers/redress_cons/greenpaper_en.pdf).

expanded the scope of consumer litigation beyond well-established avenues of consumer protection. Based on a massive data collection effort that identified important CPA statutes and decisions in federal district and state appellate courts from 2000 to 2007, the Searle Civil Justice Institute (2009) found that the (absolute) increase in CPA litigation exceeded the increase in tort litigation and that the value of recovery for potential plaintiffs (and their lawyers) had increased dramatically.

Lawyers also engage with the political and regulatory processes to influence policymakers to maintain the status quo if policy reforms may be harmful to both their and their clients' interests and to adopt new policies that may advance those interests. We discuss lawyers' behavior as an influential interest group in detail later; we note here two recent examples. Attorneys from more than twenty law firms met extensively with commissioners from the federal Commodity Futures Trading Commission to shape the implementation of new financial regulations under the Dodd-Frank Wall Street Reform and Consumer Protection Act.[12] Lawyers have also taken steps to block health care reform measures that would limit attorneys' fees or impose caps on damages in medical malpractice cases.

Finally, Barton (2007) argues that lawyers' incomes have been favorably affected by judges' systematic rulings that have enabled lawyers to be entirely self-regulated, that have restricted advertising competition, and that have limited entry into the legal profession.

Lawyers' Earnings

Previous researchers analyzing the market for lawyers also noted that their supply is constrained by the available space at law schools. Pashigian (1977) concluded that the sharp rise in the real earnings of lawyers in the 1960s created a disequilibrium that would have required a 17 to 19 percent increase in their number to restore equilibrium. Subsequently, Rosen (1992) found that the supply of lawyers increased sufficiently in the 1970s to eliminate, by the early 1980s,

12. Jenna Greene, "Hot Commodity," *National Law Journal*, October 25, 2010.

much of the market disequilibrium that Pashigian had identified. Sander and Williams (1989) summarized the population of lawyers and the national income generated by legal services through the late 1980s. We are not aware, however, of more recent quantitative analyses of the market for lawyers or estimates of the share of national income flowing to lawyers over time.[13]

Because lawyers are employed widely throughout the economy, not simply in establishments specializing in legal services, any estimate of aggregate lawyer earnings must be constructed using data from surveys or a census of individual incomes. We obtain estimates for the thirty-year period 1975–2004 of the number and average income of practicing lawyers in the United States who work in law firms, the government, and the rest of the private sector.

Three reliable, albeit imperfect, sources of data can be used to estimate the number of lawyers nationwide: the Current Population Survey (CPS), the American Bar Association, and the decennial Census of Population. We rely primarily on the CPS data because we also use them to estimate average earnings.[14] The CPS is a monthly survey of households. The March survey includes detailed questions for each member of the household, including questions relating to age, education, occupation, and all forms of income. The survey now includes about 60,000 U.S. households, and the specific households that are surveyed change over time. As a result, its estimates of the number of workers and average wages in a given occupation are subject to sampling error. Moreover, the CPS does not provide a panel of data that can be used to glean how individuals adjust to changes in economic conditions. Nevertheless, the estimates of the number of lawyers that emerge from the annual CPS surveys roughly track the ABA data through the 1970s until the early 1990s. Thereafter, the estimates of the number of lawyers that emerge from the CPS fall somewhat below the ABA's esti-

13. Lueck, Olsen, and Ransom (1995) focused on interstate differences in licensing lawyers using data up to 1988.

14. We have selected "earnings" or "earned income" as the appropriate measure for our analysis because those categories capture wages for salaried lawyers and self-income for self-employed lawyers. Earnings do not include any investment, dividend, or rental income.

mates.[15] The CPS estimates track the decennial census estimates very closely for 1979 and 1999 but are substantially below the 1989 census estimate. Both the ABA and the CPS data indicate that almost three-fourths of lawyers are employed by law firms—the "legal services" industry—with the remainder employed by other firms in the private sector or by the government.[16]

The number of lawyers in the United States, based on the CPS data, is shown in figure 2-2. This number nearly doubled from 1975 to 1990, but the recent growth in lawyers has been much slower, with the number increasing roughly 20 percent since 1990.[17] As of 2004 about 900,000 lawyers were in practice, with nearly 650,000 working in law firms or as sole proprietors and a somewhat greater share of the remaining lawyers working in government than in other private firms. Despite recent reports of a sharp decline in the demand for lawyers stemming from the recession that began in late 2007, legal-services employment has held up remarkably well. According to the Bureau of Labor Statistics, the number of persons employed in "legal occupations" actually rose from 1.67 million in 2007 to 1.72 million in 2010.[18] The employment of lawyers rose from 1.00 million to 1.14 million during the same period, although the top 250 firms have shed some 5,200 attorneys. By contrast, employment in several other professions, such as architects, mechanical engineers, and dentists actually declined somewhat, and the number of persons employed as "chief executives" declined sharply—from 1.70 million in 2007 to 1.50 million in 2010.

15. A discrepancy between the ABA and the CPS estimates may exist because the ABA tracks the "number of licensed lawyers," while the CPS reports survey individuals' main occupation in a given year. Thus the ABA estimates may exceed the CPS estimates because some lawyers have gone into another line of work or have retired but have kept their license.

16. To facilitate comparisons across years and across surveys, judges are added together with lawyers in both the CPS and decennial census samples because they are indistinguishable from lawyers in the CPS starting with the 1995 survey. Judges typically represent about 4 percent of the sample in a given year.

17. According to the Law School Admission Council, law school seats expanded much more rapidly in the 1970s than in the more recent period.

18. As reported in the *Wall Street Journal*'s online edition (http://online. wsj.com/article/SB10001424052748703791904576075652301620440.html).

Figure 2-2. *Number of U.S. Lawyers by Sector, 1975–2004*

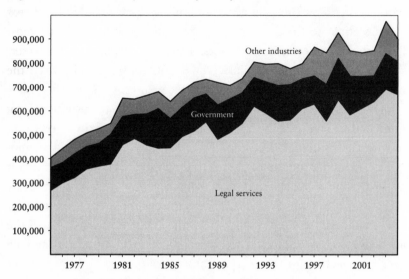

Source: U.S. Census Bureau, Current Population Survey.

Because the CPS censors data on incomes for the highest income earners, it must be supplemented with other data to obtain an estimate of lawyers' aggregate earnings. The upper limits (for example, survey respondents in a given year are asked whether they make $100,000 or more than that amount) for reported annual earned income from a worker's primary job have varied over time: the limit was $50,000 from 1975 through 1980; $75,000 in 1981–83; $99,999 in 1984–1994; $150,000 in 1995–2001; and $200,000 in 2002–2004. All limits are in nominal dollars. We can obtain uncensored earnings of lawyers employed in the legal services industry—defined as corporations, partnerships, and sole proprietorships whose principal output is legal services—from estimates of "value added" in legal services, produced by the Bureau of Economic Analysis (BEA). Those data exclude the earnings of lawyers in other firms and in government.[19]

19. As noted, fewer than 30 percent of all lawyers are employed outside the legal services industry.

Given that law firms are owned by some or all of the lawyers who work in them, we can assume that all of the value added in law firms accrues either to the employees of the firms, both lawyers and non-lawyers, or to their lawyer owners. Thus, the earnings of lawyers in those establishments can be calculated as the difference between the BEA value-added estimates of legal-services enterprises and their non-lawyer labor costs. The latter costs are calculated as the product of the number and average earnings of nonlawyers in this sector as reported in annual CPS data.[20]

Uncensored estimates of the average earnings of lawyers in the rest of the private sector and in government are not available.[21] We therefore assume that the effect of CPS censoring of the average earnings of lawyers in legal services is the same as the effect of its censoring of the average earnings of lawyers in those two sectors. We determine CPS censoring factors for the average earnings of lawyers in legal services by inflating each censored observation in the CPS legal services sample by an amount that equates the CPS estimate of aggregate earnings to the (uncensored) BEA estimate of aggregate earnings. (For some specific years the censored CPS estimates of average earnings had to be more than doubled.) We then apply annual adjustment factors to all censored observations in the CPS samples for lawyers in the rest of the private sector and in government to determine their average annual earnings. This procedure may overstate aggregate earnings somewhat if government lawyers with censored reported incomes in the CPS tend to earn less than private legal services lawyers with censored incomes.

20. Those data are uncensored because average wages of secretaries, para-legals, mailroom clerks, and other nonlawyers who work at law firms tend to be substantially below the highest thresholds established by the CPS over time.

21. Although the U.S. Census provides the mean value of each source of income for individuals whose income is top-coded, or censored, we cannot make use of those cell means to eliminate the downward bias in calculating the average income of lawyers from annual CPS data because they reflect the average of top-coded incomes over a variety of occupations (Burkhauser, Feng, and Jenkins 2007). Unfortunately, publicly available cell means for the sources of income for lawyers and for other specific occupations do not exist.

Figure 2-3. *Aggregate Real Compensation of Lawyers, 1975–2004*

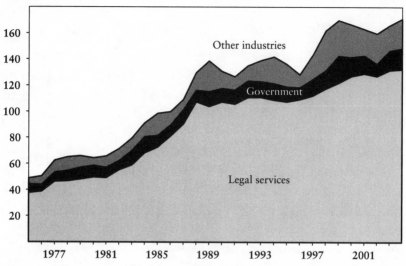

Billions of 2005$

Source: U.S. Census Bureau, Current Population Survey.

However, the group of government lawyers with censored incomes only makes up 3 percent of the national lawyer population.

We can obtain an estimate of the aggregate earnings of lawyers in the United States from 1975 through 2004 by multiplying for each sector the (BEA-adjusted) average earnings of lawyers by the number of lawyers and summing the totals. The results, shown in figure 2-3, indicate that real earnings have grown substantially over the sample period, but they grew much faster between 1975 and 1990 (6.6 percent annually) than between 1990 and 2004 (less than 2 percent annually).[22] Lawyers in the legal services sector, that is, law firms, now account for roughly 77 percent of lawyers' income. By 2004 the United States was spending $170 billion on lawyers (in 2005 dollars), which represented nearly 1.5 percent of gross domestic product. Note that this estimate does not include spending on the related costs of legal services, including the cost of workers who assist attorneys, such as

22. We report real estimates in 2005 dollars using the consumer price index from the Bureau of Labor Statistics.

Figure 2-4. *The Changing Distribution of Lawyers' Incomes,
1975–2004*[a]

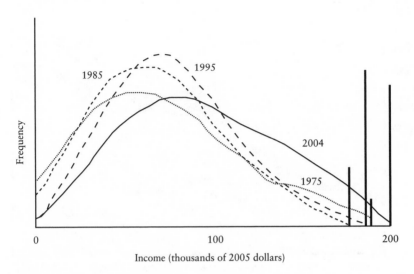

Income (thousands of 2005 dollars)

Source: Authors' calculations based on the Current Population Survey.

a. Kernel density estimates of the distributions of lawyers' incomes are constructed using the earnings data of lawyers in the Current Population Survey (CPS) for the years 1975, 1985, 1995, and 2004, respectively. All incomes are inflated to constant 2005 dollars using the consumer price index for urban consumers from the U.S. Bureau of Labor Statistics. The density estimates are smoothed using the Epanechnikov kernel. The share of censored lawyers' incomes as represented by the narrow bars is approximately 3, 6, 22, and 18 percent of the sample for 1975, 1985, 1995, and 2004, respectively

secretaries, paralegals, and consultants. And despite the recession that began in 2007, crude estimates in market research reports suggest that as of 2010 the United States was still spending some $200 billion a year on lawyers.

The growth in lawyers' real earnings does not appear to be confined to a small, select group of lawyers. Figure 2-4 uses data from the CPS to present changes in the distribution of lawyers' incomes from 1975 to 2004. Real average incomes have risen over time as indicated by the consistent rightward shift in the distributions. Lawyers with the lowest earnings have enjoyed increases in their incomes throughout the period, as indicated by the shrinking left tail of the distributions. And lawyers with the highest earnings also have raised their incomes significantly, as indicated by the increasing mass of legal professionals at the far right tail of the distributions whose incomes meet CPS censoring thresholds.

Despite recent concerns about the job market for lawyers, employment in the legal profession has not declined in the aftermath of the recession, and any decrease in the number of law school applicants over previous years will not prevent the profession from filling the ranks of retirees. We now begin our investigation of whether the prospect of sizable earnings premiums may be part of the profession's appeal.

CHAPTER THREE

Evidence of Earnings Premiums in the Legal Profession

Previous research provides some empirical evidence that lawyers receive earnings premiums, but this research does not attempt to fully resolve the methodological debate of whether those premiums may simply reflect unobserved skills, abilities, and working conditions. Looking at new entrants to the legal profession, Pagliero (2010) concludes that lawyers' salaries increase as bar examination pass rates decrease. He also concludes, however, that lower pass rates are not associated with higher-quality lawyers, which suggests that the higher salaries reflect premiums that are unrelated to ability. Rebitzer and Taylor (1995) provide some corroborating evidence rejecting the hypothesis that associates at large law firms are paid efficiency wages to elicit higher productivity and finding instead that those associates receive substantial earnings premiums. Tenn (2001) reports evidence that stricter licensing statutes, which are not correlated with measures of higher worker quality, lead to higher wages for lawyers. And Brickman (forthcoming); McKee, Santore, and Shelton (2007); and Santore and Viard (2001) conclude from research on contingency fees charged by lawyers in tort liability cases that those attorneys are receiving earnings premiums. Brickman (2004) estimates that total annual premiums earned by tort lawyers alone approached $7 billion in the early 2000s.

A simple international comparison of the average number of lawyers per capita and lawyers' average annual earnings raises the question whether lawyers working in the United States earn premiums. As shown in table 3-1, the United States has many more lawyers per capita than all but a few countries in the world; only Greece reports more. This fact by itself appears to argue against the claim that ABA regulations are restricting the supply of lawyers—until one considers lawyers' earnings. Data on average lawyer incomes throughout the developed world are somewhat scarce, but table 3-2 reports the fragmentary evidence that Clark (2002) has extracted from a variety of institutional and scholarly sources. The table also includes other estimates that we were able to obtain from published sources. Even though the United States has more practicing lawyers per capita than virtually any other country, the average annual income of these lawyers greatly exceeds average annual lawyer incomes elsewhere in the world (in U.S. dollars at current exchange rates for the years cited).

The income differences could be attributable to supply restrictions because, even though the United States has more lawyers per capita than other countries, its supply should possibly be even greater, given the extensive legal work in the country. Another way of looking at the matter is that as a society thought to be litigious, the United States tends to institute policies that increase the demand for lawyers. As an interest group, lawyers may promote such policies. Of course, the differences could reflect other factors such as international variations in the structure of legal services.

The case of Japan is potentially useful for suggesting that earnings premiums in the United States could be generated by differences in supply and demand between the United States and other countries. Nakazato, Ramseyer, and Rasmusen (2007) point out that the Japanese government requires all individuals who aspire to practice law in Japan to study at its Legal Research and Training Institute. But to do so requires passing an entrance exam with a historical acceptance rate of only 3 percent! The Japanese government has recently tried to increase the number of lawyers in Japan by establishing new law

Table 3-1. *Number of Lawyers per 1,000 Population, 2006*

Country	Number of lawyers	Population	Lawyers per 1,000 persons
Austria	4,234	8,254,000	0.51
Belgium	6,727	10,511,000	0.64
Canada	72,000	32,649,000	2.21
Cyprus	1,025	766,000	1.34
Czech Republic	7,729	10,251,000	0.75
Denmark	4,901	5,427,000	0.90
Finland	1,761	5,256,000	0.34
France	45,686	63,229,000	0.72
Germany	138,679	82,438,000	1.68
Greece	36,000	11,125,000	3.24
Hungary	9,717	10,077,000	0.96
Ireland	1,156	4,209,000	0.27
Italy	121,380	58,752,000	2.07
Japan	22,000	127,756,000	0.17
Latvia	992	2,295,000	0.43
Lithuania	999	3,403,000	0.29
Luxembourg	1,262	469,000	2.69
Netherlands	14,251	16,334,000	0.87
Norway	5,390	4,611,000	1.17
Poland	8,488	38,157,000	0.22
Portugal	12,617	10,570,000	1.19
Romania	16,998	21,610,000	0.79
Slovak Republic	4,302	5,389,000	0.80
Slovenia	687	2,003,000	0.34
Spain	114,143	43,758,000	2.61
Sweden	4,415	9,048,000	0.49
Switzerland	7,710	7,459,000	1.03
United Kingdom	151,043	60,393,000	2.50
United States (2004)	900,000	293,655,000	3.06

Sources: Council of Bars and Law Societies of Europe; Australian Bureau of Statistics; "Japan: Lawyers Wanted. No, Really," *Business Week*, April 3, 2006; U.S. Census Bureau, Current Population Survey.

schools and offering a new national bar exam. But the pass rate is still low—roughly 40 percent in 2007. Despite this formidable entry barrier to legal practice, which appears to exceed the barrier to practice law in the United States, Kinoshita (2000) concludes that lawyers in

Table 3-2. *Average Private Lawyer Earnings in Selected Countries*
U.S.$ at current exchange rates for the years cited

Country	Year	Average earnings	
Australia	1989	Queen's counsel	112,000
		Barrister	48,000
		Solicitor partner	54,000
		Solicitor employee	30,000
Australia	2002	All lawyers	90,000
Canada (Toronto only)	1990	Male lawyer	154,000
		Female lawyer	106,000
Canada	2002	All lawyers	64,000
Switzerland	1982	All lawyers	113,552
Italy	1990	All lawyers	16,800
Japan	1990	All bengoshi	155,000
Japan	2000	All lawyers	146,000
United Kingdom	1980s	Queen's counsel	98,000
		Partners (solicitors)	66,000
		Junior lawyers	25,000–57,000
United States	1990	Lawyers in law firms	132,000
United States	2000	Lawyers in law firms	191,000

Sources: All data are from Clark (2002), except for Japan 2000 (Nakazato, Ramseyer, and Rasmusen 2007) and United States 2000 (U.S. Census Bureau, Current Population Survey, and U.S. Department of Commerce, Bureau of Economic Analysis).

Japan earn modest incomes and are prevented by regulation from earning higher incomes.[1] Furthermore, after accounting for the expense and opportunity cost of a legal education and the probability of receiving the required training, the expected rate of return on human capital investment in law is very low in Japan. One explanation may be that Japan allows some 90,000 scriveners and other workers, many of whom have undergraduate law degrees, to do much of the ordinary tax, patent, administrative, and real estate work that is done in the United States by higher-priced attorneys.[2]

1. As table 3-2 indicates, Japanese lawyer incomes, while relatively high compared with those in many other advanced countries, were clearly below those in the United States in 2000.
2. S. Chang and J. D. Reed, "Land without Lawyers," *Time*, August 1, 1983.

Ramseyer (1986) suggests that lawyers in Japan may be a less successful interest group than are lawyers in the United States because regulation of the legal services industry in Japan reflects the interests of the government and major consumers of those services more than the interests of members of the bar. Accordingly, lawyers in Japan may also be less successful than lawyers in the United States at increasing government-induced demand.

In the remainder of this chapter, we begin the process of developing evidence that U.S. lawyers receive earnings premiums that are unrelated to skills or other personal characteristics. We estimate earnings equations based on data in the (March) Current Population Survey (CPS) from 1975 to 2004 to determine the earnings premiums accruing to lawyers and to individuals working in other occupations in the United States. At this point, we do not indicate whether such premiums reflect efficiencies or inefficient labor market restrictions because any premiums could reflect unobserved abilities and skills of individuals who self-select to join that occupation—that is, the premiums could reflect selectivity bias—as well as unobserved characteristics of the occupation. If lawyers' estimated premiums do reflect unobserved job characteristics, abilities, or skills, calling them inefficient would be erroneous.

Our approach, following the standard approach in labor economics developed by Katz and Summers (1989), is to specify an individual's annual earnings as a function of supply and demand factors along with occupational dummy variables. In such an earnings regression, the coefficients on the occupational dummy variables should capture the earnings premiums enjoyed by workers in their respective occupations. However, as Katz and Summers (p. 210) were careful to point out, it would be incautious to assume that the occupational dummies are reflecting inefficiencies when they may be capturing interindustry wage differentials, which may also be explained by competitive factors such as differences in skill or working conditions.

The standard way to control for unobserved individual characteristics, such as skills and abilities, would be to specify individual fixed effects in a model estimated on a longitudinal sample of workers. But, as noted, the CPS sample does not include the same individuals in each year. And even if it did, Gibbons and others (2005) point out that individual fixed effects would be perfectly correlated with the occupational dummies except for respondents who switch occupations—a small minority in the case of lawyers. As an additional concern, those respondents who switch occupations may be influenced to do so by unobserved stimuli that are correlated with ability, skills, or circumstances that may in turn bias estimates of earnings premiums.[3]

Another approach would be to treat the occupational dummies as endogenous and jointly estimate them along with the coefficients in the earnings equation. But this approach is hampered by the lack of suitable instruments—that is, variables that would be correlated with an individual's choice of occupation but uncorrelated with the individual's earnings. For example, if we estimated an earnings equation using spousal characteristics, such as age, education, and occupation, as instruments for the occupational dummies, it could be argued that a basic theory of household formation and bargaining would imply that those characteristics would necessarily correlate with an individual's earnings.[4]

Thus, in the absence of a single persuasive econometric approach applied to an empirical model, we conduct several piecemeal robustness tests, sometimes using alternative data sources to the CPS, to test whether the occupational dummies are solely reflecting lawyers' working conditions, areas of specialization, abilities, and returns to skills. None of the tests on their own is dispositive, but we believe that their repeated finding that lawyers' earnings premiums cannot be explained by those factors provides compelling evidence that the premiums reflect inefficiencies in the market for lawyers—that is, restrictions on the supply of new entrants to the profession. A final potential issue is

---

3. The American Community Survey of households is another survey we could potentially use, but it begins only after the 2000 Census and thus does not allow us to analyze lawyers' earnings premiums over time.

4. Gibbons and others (2005) used instruments as a robustness check on their estimate of the standard deviation of occupational rents across industries, but they did not use instrumental variables to obtain point estimates of specific occupational dummy variables.

that distinguishing between occupational earnings premiums versus industry earnings premiums may be difficult, but in this case, the distinction should be minimal because lawyers in private law firms account for the bulk of activity in the legal services industry.

Specification and Estimation of the Earnings Equations

Because we want to capture the annual variation in occupational earnings premiums, we estimate separate earnings equations for each of the years 1975–2004 using individuals' income and socioeconomic variables from the unadjusted CPS. The dependent variable is the natural logarithm of earned income (before deductions) from an individual's primary job. As noted in chapter 2, one problem is that the CPS income data are censored for individuals with income above a certain threshold value, with the upper limits varying over time.[5]

Two approaches have been employed to address this censoring problem. One, used by Rosen (1992), for example, is to estimate the values of the censored observations by tobit regression and then to use those estimated values in least squares regressions for the entire sample; the other, used by Katz and Murphy (1992) and by Autor, Katz, and Kearney (2005), is to multiply the income of those with censored income data by 1.5—a figure based on an analysis of a confidential subsample of the CPS that reported incomes for even high-earning respondents. We estimate our earnings equations using tobit regression and perform a sensitivity analysis by estimating the earnings equations by least squares after multiplying censored incomes by 1.5. We perform additional sensitivity analysis when we estimate an earnings equation using data from the Panel Study of Income Dynamics, which does not censor individuals' earnings.

5. Before the 1996 survey (capturing 1995 income), all censored values were reported as the upper limit. Beginning in 1996, however, the CPS reported censored incomes as the average of all observations above the upper limit for all persons in a given demographic group. The number of such groups has varied over time. From 1975 through 1980 the upper limit was $50,000; in 1981–83, $75,000; in 1984–94, $99,999; in 1995–2001, $150,000; and in 2002–04, $200,000. All upper limits are reported in nominal dollars.

Sixteen occupation dummies are used, including one for lawyers, to estimate the earnings premiums. Among the sixteen are occupations that have significant entry barriers that might generate earnings premiums as well as occupations with no entry barriers and minimal skill requirements and that would be expected to have earnings premiums below most other occupations. The occupations not specified in the model serve as the "base" occupations, and their earnings premiums are assumed to be zero to provide a quantitative interpretation to the occupational dummy variables for lawyers. We subject that interpretation to sensitivity analysis by reestimating our earnings equations using alternative base occupations and by comparing our estimates with others in the literature. We are primarily interested in the behavior of the occupational dummy variables for lawyers over time, which is less sensitive to the choice of base occupations.

The supply factors included are socioeconomic characteristics of the individuals in the sample—sex, race, education level, work experience (which incorporates age), and employment status (full time or part time).[6] These variables are broadly aligned with those included in an index of observed skills developed by Gibbons and others (2005).[7]

The demand factors that would be expected to influence earnings are industry output per worker and a measure of technology such as the capital-labor ratio.[8] In our context, however, it would be inap-

6. There may be concern that employment status is endogenous; but this variable has been found in other contexts to be strongly determined by scheduling flexibility rather than earnings, especially for women. In any case, our findings were not affected when this variable was omitted from the model.

7. Gibbons and colleagues also estimate their wage equation with an expanded skill index, including the Armed Forces Qualifying Test (AFQT) score, as a broad measure of premarket skills. This score is not included in the CPS, but the authors' findings are quite similar for models using the skill index with and without the AFQT.

8. Another demand-related variable we initially included in the specification was a dummy variable for import-intensive industries, based on data from the National Bureau of Economic Research, to control for the extent of foreign competition. Lawrence and Slaughter (1993) point out that imports and exports may affect wages. They controlled for both effects and found that trade was not an important contributor to U.S. average wages.

propriate to hold those variables constant because they are affected by exogenous influences that may create earnings premiums. That is, if constraints on the number of available law school seats contribute to earnings premiums by reducing labor in the legal services sector, then output per worker and the capital-labor ratio would capture this effect, thereby reducing the estimated coefficient for earnings premiums in the legal profession. At the same time, certain exogenous changes in government policy may increase the demand for lawyers and contribute to earnings premiums, but that effect may be difficult to capture because the number of lawyers (and changes in the distribution of lawyers' specializations) is constrained. Selectivity bias would affect the quality of lawyers but not their (constrained) quantity, which is primarily what the denominator of the demand variables is measuring. In any case, the demand variables are not included in the initial estimations, but we later report estimates of positive occupational earnings premiums to lawyers based on specifications that include those variables.

As noted, we are interested in the effect of government-induced demand on lawyers' premiums, which may result from certain public policies that are difficult to specify in this specification. In the next chapter, we explore the possibility that the effect of those policies on lawyers' earnings may be captured by the occupational dummy variables for lawyers.

Finally, we include regional dummy variables defined by census region to capture all omitted regional influences on earnings. The regions are New England, Middle Atlantic, East North Central, West North Central, South Atlantic, East South Central, West South Central, Mountain, and Pacific.

Estimation results for the selected years 1975, 1985, 1995, and 2004 are presented in table 3-3. The parameter estimates of the socioeconomic variables are generally significant and have reasonable signs. Consistent with other research, the coefficients suggest that the returns from higher education have increased over time and that either wage discrimination against women in the workforce has decreased over time or certain unobserved differences in job selection may have

Table 3-3. *Tobit Maximum-Likelihood Estimates of Individual Earnings, Selected Years*[a]

Independent variable	1975	1985	1995	2004
Education dummy (1 if high school completed, 0 otherwise)[b]	0.2041 (0.0058)	0.2573 (0.0066)	0.2876 (0.0080)	0.3363 (0.0643)
Education dummy (1 if college completed, 0 otherwise)[b]	0.2714 (0.0062)	0.3079 (0.0052)	0.3586 (0.0060)	0.3923 (0.0046)
Education dummy (1 if advanced/ professional degree completed, 0 otherwise)[b]	0.1563 (0.0093)	0.1720 (0.0077)	0.2022 (0.0092)	0.1970 (0.0069)
Years of work experience[c]	0.0309 (0.0005)	0.0326 (0.0005)	0.0309 (0.0006)	0.0278 (0.0005)
Years of work experience squared[c]	−0.0005 (0.0000+)	−0.0005 (0.0000+)	−0.0005 (0.0000+)	−0.0004 (0.0000+)
Female dummy (1 if female, 0 otherwise)	−0.4275 (0.0044)	−0.3409 (0.0040)	−0.2620 (0.0047)	−0.2386 (0.0037)
Race (1 if black, 0 otherwise)[d]	−0.1101 (0.0072)	−0.1407 (0.0066)	−0.1038 (0.0075)	−0.1028 (0.0058)
Race (1 if not black or white, 0 otherwise)[d]	−0.0960 (0.0162)	−0.1187 (0.0118)	−0.0913 (0.0115)	−0.0619 (0.0072)
Work status dummy (1 if worked part time during year, 0 otherwise)	−0.4225 (0.0080)	−0.4250 (0.0074)	−0.3699 (0.0085)	−0.4005 (0.0066)
Work status dummy (1 if worked part of the year, 0 otherwise)	−0.3604 (0.0049)	−0.3517 (0.0051)	−0.2893 (0.0067)	−0.2982 (0.0056)

Geographical dummies (1 if household is in given region, 0 otherwise)[e]

Middle Atlantic	0.0599 (0.0097)	0.0053 (0.0091)	0.0255 (0.0113)	−0.0053 (0.0091)
East North Central	0.0722 (0.0095)	0.0026 (0.0091)	0.0044 (0.0110)	−0.0318 (0.0090)
West North Central	−0.0105 (0.0111)	−0.0757 (0.0106)	−0.0827 (0.0127)	−0.0723 (0.0102)
South Atlantic	−0.0142 (0.0099)	−0.0601 (0.0091)	−0.0538 (0.0110)	−0.0451 (0.0088)
East South Central	−0.0734 (0.0117)	−0.1457 (0.0113)	−0.0914 (0.0134)	−0.0867 (0.0109)
West South Central	−0.0402 (0.0106)	−0.0282 (0.0098)	−0.0794 (0.0119)	−0.0773 (0.0095)
Mountain	0.0049 (0.0127)	−0.0356 (0.0113)	−0.0658 (0.0133)	−0.0681 (0.0103)
Pacific	0.0793 (0.0100)	0.0386 (0.0092)	0.0293 (0.0112)	0.0156 (0.0090)

(continued)

Table 3-3. *Tobit Maximum-Likelihood Estimates of Individual Earnings, Selected Years*[a] *(continued)*

Independent variable	1975	1985	1995	2004
Occupational dummies (1 if individual is employed in given occupation, 0 otherwise)[f]				
Architect	0.1008	–0.0281	0.0877	0.0398
	(0.0660)	(0.0547)	(0.0575)	(0.0415)
Dentist	0.4673	0.4012	0.5757	0.7741
	(0.0554)	(0.0506)	(0.0678)	(0.0511)
Industrial engineer	0.2186	0.2374	0.1403	0.3065
	(0.0391)	(0.0404)	(0.0475)	(0.0428)
Mechanical engineer	0.2631	0.2377	0.2597	0.3012
	(0.0376)	(0.0344)	(0.0412)	(0.0359)
Pharmacist	0.0814	0.1159	0.3040	0.5549
	(0.0522)	(0.0427)	(0.0558)	(0.0427)
Physician	0.6047	0.5123	0.6155	0.7092
	(0.0302)	(0.0273)	(0.0305)	(0.0241)
Economist	0.2015	0.1091	0.1681	0.5233
	(0.0555)	(0.0593)	(0.0580)	(0.1003)
Elementary school teacher	0.0147	–0.0522	–0.0354	–0.1258
	(0.0154)	(0.0165)	(0.0183)	(0.0129)
Insurance agent	0.0855	0.1103	0.1941	0.1135
	(0.0243)	(0.0254)	(0.0294)	(0.0270)
Real estate agent	0.0250	0.1132	0.1338	0.1996
	(0.0300)	(0.0242)	(0.0275)	(0.0226)
Financial services sales agent	0.2795	0.3067	0.3256	0.3888
	(0.0591)	(0.0362)	(0.0380)	(0.0314)
Electrician	0.2193	0.1127	0.0842	0.0963
	(0.0227)	(0.0227)	(0.0272)	(0.0215)
Bus driver	–0.0552	–0.0872	–0.1750	–0.1657
	(0.0353)	(0.0332)	(0.0373)	(0.0299)
Waiter	–0.2544	–0.2029	–0.2159	–0.2693
	(0.0247)	(0.0220)	(0.0292)	(0.0202)
Farmer	–0.4035	–0.4294	–0.3012	–0.3465
	(0.0244)	(0.0277)	(0.0336)	(0.0266)
Lawyer	0.2588	0.3004	0.3619	0.4898
	(0.0291)	(0.0240)	(0.0273)	(0.0218)
Constant	8.819	9.4040	9.6289	9.8902
	(0.0111)	(0.0111)	(0.0136)	(0.0110)

Table 3-3. *Tobit Maximum-Likelihood Estimates of Individual Earnings, Selected Years[a] (continued)*

Item	1975	1985	1995	2004
Number of observations	45,042	58,334	49,061	82,341
Number of censored observations	307	391	505	986
Log likelihood	−26373	−42244	−39650	−72618
Pseudo R^2	0.3561	0.2714	0.2124	0.2032

Source: Authors' calculations.

   a. Dependent variable: Natural logarithm of year's income (before deductions) from an individual's primary job. Standard errors in parentheses.

   b.The education variables should be interpreted as having marginal effects.

   c. Following Katz and Murphy (1992), years of work experience is defined as age minus years of education (constructed from the CPS record on education) minus 7.

   d. The base race is white.

   e. Coefficients of geographical dummies are relative to a base of the excluded New England dummy variable.

   f. Coefficients of occupational dummies are relative to all occupations other than the sixteen occupations for which there are dummy variables.

changed over time. In addition, the relative returns from a high school, college, and graduate school education appear to be plausible, with the highest marginal returns produced by an undergraduate education.[9] The occupational dummies indicate that individuals in several occupations that require workers to obtain a license or some form of cer-

   9. We specify the graduate school dummy variable by combining the completion of an advanced (for example, PhD) or professional (for example, JD) degree. This variable mixes different graduate degrees, but we found that specifying three dummy variables for master's, doctorate, and professional degrees had little effect on the estimates of occupational earnings premiums. Black, Sanders, and Taylor (2003) have raised concerns that survey respondents do not accurately report whether they have received a graduate degree, often claiming to have completed such a degree when in fact they have not. The authors assess the decennial census, the National Survey of College Graduates (NSCG), and the CPS. However, they point out that the CPS is conducted with trained interviewers who can and do ask follow-up questions to eliminate bias; such questions check for inconsistencies in a respondent's answers over time and inconsistencies between the respondent's age and when the respondent claimed to have obtained a degree. Moreover, the authors acknowledge that they have no method to identify bias in responses in the CPS sample.

tification before they can legally serve the public—including law, medicine, dentistry, pharmacy, engineering, and financial services—are receiving high earnings premiums compared with those obtained by workers in other occupations. At the same time, workers in occupations with either very modest or no entry barriers, including driving a bus, serving food at restaurants, and farming, and workers in occupations that are known for their low salaries, such as elementary school teachers, earn premiums that are below those of workers in other occupations. Thus the relative estimates of the occupational dummies in the model are broadly consistent with our assumption that the earnings premiums for the base occupations are equal to zero.

The Growth and Distribution of Lawyers' Earnings Premiums

The occupational coefficients for lawyers from 1975 to 2004, presented in table 3-4, show our estimates of the growth in lawyers' earnings premiums. The first column of the table presents coefficients that were estimated using a tobit regression. Although the coefficients fluctuate mildly from year to year, they clearly indicate lawyers' earnings premiums have increased over time—hovering at around 25 percent during the latter part of the 1970s and rising to about 50 percent in more recent years. We explore the possible sources of the increase in premiums later.

This quantitative interpretation is based on the sixteen occupational dummies included in the specification and on the assumption that the earnings premium of the base occupations is equal to zero. As a sensitivity analysis, we estimated two alternative earnings models, one that included five additional, randomly chosen occupations and one that included the ten most common occupations not included among the initial sixteen. In both alternative models, we found that the coefficients of the occupational dummy for lawyers changed very little quantitatively from their values in the original model.

Kleiner and Krueger (2010) found that occupational licensing across all occupations was associated with a 15 percent increase in wages, all else equal. We expect that the increase in lawyers' earnings

Table 3-4. *Earnings Premiums of Lawyers, Physicians, and Dentists, 1975–2004*

Premium as a share of average income

| Year | Lawyers | | | Physicians | Dentists |
	Tobit: without Q/L and K/L	OLS: inflating censored income 1.5	Tobit: including Q/L and K/L	Tobit: without Q/L and K/L	Tobit: without Q/L and K/L
1975	0.259	0.274	0.122	0.605	0.467
1976	0.315	0.342	0.172	0.679	0.627
1977	0.258	0.288	0.101	0.573	0.666
1978	0.252	0.277	0.115	0.608	0.702
1979	0.319	0.354	0.174	0.544	0.545
1980	0.262	0.292	0.121	0.479	0.393
1981	0.276	0.291	0.147	0.529	0.433
1982	0.287	0.312	0.141	0.562	0.413
1983	0.316	0.334	0.174	0.549	0.489
1984	0.267	0.273	0.135	0.515	0.382
1985	0.300	0.315	0.169	0.512	0.401
1986	0.354	0.378	0.207	0.609	0.501
1987	0.381	0.394	0.240	0.530	0.379
1988	0.418	0.440	0.243	0.565	0.455
1989	0.410	0.425	0.261	0.570	0.514
1990	0.499	0.515	0.333	0.573	0.556
1991	0.413	0.434	0.248	0.610	0.514
1992	0.515	0.541	0.346	0.550	0.495
1993	0.539	0.569	0.371	0.594	0.586
1994	0.392	0.410	0.233	0.713	0.612
1995	0.362	0.373	0.180	0.615	0.576
1996	0.413	0.425	0.244	0.579	0.475
1997	0.385	0.402	0.224	0.633	0.653
1998	0.444	0.468	0.312	0.579	0.600
1999	0.390	0.407	0.246	0.646	0.654
2000	0.504	0.519	0.348	0.600	0.530
2001	0.425	0.442	0.272	0.625	0.622
2002	0.413	0.431	0.296	0.749	0.632
2003	0.555	0.582	0.430	0.693	0.685
2004	0.490	0.511	0.366	0.709	0.774

Source: Authors' calculations.

Note: All coefficient estimates are statistically significant at the 1 percent confidence level. Q/L = output per worker; K/L = capital/labor ratio. OLS= ordinary least squares.

should clearly exceed this average—as it does in our estimates—because lawyers' earnings are increased by entry restrictions on firms and the increased demand for legal services caused by government actions as well as by occupational licensing. Indeed, Kleiner (2006) assesses the impact of licensing (and implicitly of the other influences just noted) on hourly wages by comparing the coefficient for lawyers with the coefficient for an unlicensed occupation, sociologists, and reports a difference of 0.454, which is consistent with our estimates.

The second column of the table indicates that the estimates of lawyers' earnings premiums are not particularly sensitive to how we correct for the truncation of earnings in the CPS sample, because the coefficients increase only slightly when we inflate individuals' earnings by 1.5 and estimate the model by least squares instead of tobit.[10] As expected, the estimates of lawyers' earnings premiums are reduced if output per worker and the capital-labor ratio are included in the earnings equation because those variables hold the supply of lawyers constant and therefore pick up entry restrictions into the legal profession that may affect earnings.[11] The third column shows that lawyers' earnings premiums drop about 15 percentage points in a given year when those variables are included, although they still increase over time. The 15 percentage point difference remains roughly constant over time, suggesting that the growth in lawyers' earnings premiums is not driven by changes in capital utilization and output per se during the period, but leaving open the possibility that the growth is influenced by changes in government policy that increase the demand for lawyers while their supply is constrained.

Finally, it is useful to compare the estimates of earnings premiums for lawyers, physicians, and dentists because those professions have

10. As noted, the expansion factor of 1.5 is based on a subsample of observations in the CPS for all occupations that does not truncate earnings.

11. We constructed output per worker and the capital-labor ratio using data from the Bureau of Economic Analysis on output, employment, and capital by industry classification. Following Katz and Murphy (1992), we constructed these variables for roughly fifty industry classifications based on SIC (standard industrial classification) codes and on NAICS (North American Industry Classification System) codes, which replaced the SIC system in 1997.

broadly similar licensing requirements that include obtaining a degree from an accredited professional school and being certified to practice by an examining board. As shown in the fourth column of table 3-4, earnings premiums for doctors are generally larger and more stable over time than those for lawyers. The relative stability of doctors' premiums is somewhat puzzling because both the medical and legal professions limit the supply of spaces in their professional schools and require certification to practice. In addition, both fields have experienced similar growth during the major period covered by our sample, 1975–2000, with the number of lawyers increasing from 442,475 to 851,234 (92.3 percent) and the number of physicians increasing from 372,736 to 730,801 (96 percent).[12]

The stability of physicians' earnings premiums could result from the involvement of third parties, such as insurers and hospitals, who may share some of their earnings premiums, and from efforts by the federal government to hold down reimbursement rates for Medicare. Dentists' earnings are less subject to third-party payments (from insurance carriers) than are physicians' earnings. As shown in the last column of table 3-4, dentists' earnings premiums declined sharply during the 1980s but then rebounded to their 1976–78 levels. This pattern does not appear to be systematically related to changes in public policy, but it is consistent with the decline in the supply of dental school graduates attributable to the closure of several dental schools during the latter part of our sample period.

Another important issue is whether the earnings premiums to lawyers accrue largely to a handful of legal superstars or are widely distributed among the legal profession. The former outcome is possible because only a small fraction of attorneys become partners at the most lucrative boutique and large law firms in the country. We estimate a quantile regression model to determine whether "occupational effects" behave differently at different points of the earnings

---

12. Data on the number of lawyers and physicians are from the CPS. Figures on the number of physicians from the *United States Health Workforce Personnel Factbook* show an increase in the number of physicians that is about 10 percent higher than the increase based on data from the CPS.

distribution—for example, does a lawyer at the top of the earnings distribution enjoy a greater level of or an increase in earnings premiums over time than a lawyer at the bottom of the earnings distribution?

Let $Q_q(y|X)$ be the qth quantile of the distribution of y conditional on the values of X. For example, for $q = 25$, $Q_{25}(y|X)$ is the 25th percentile of y conditional on the values of X, or 25 percent of the values of y are less than or equal to the specified function of X. The quantile regression model is expressed as:

$$Q_q\left(y|X\right)=\beta_0\left(q\right)+\beta_1\left(q\right)X_1+\beta_2\left(q\right)X_2+\dots+\beta_n\left(q\right)X_n+\varepsilon\left(q\right), \qquad (3\text{-}1)$$

where $\beta_j(q)$ is the parameter for the jth independent variable at quantile q and ε is an error term. Note the parameters vary with the quantile q. Estimation of the parameters at a given quantile is achieved by minimizing the sum of the absolute value of the residual terms, with each residual term weighted by an asymmetric function of q (Koenker and Basset 1978).

We reestimated all of the earnings equations, as specified in table 3-3, at various quantiles of the earnings distribution, accounting for censoring of the top-coded values by multiplying them by 1.5. Table 3-5 presents estimates of lawyers' earnings premiums for selected years at the 25th, 50th, 75th, and 90th percentiles of the earnings distribution.[13] Note that only a small share of lawyers had incomes that were top coded. The estimates of lawyers' earnings premiums exhibit little variation over much of the earnings distribution. To be sure, lawyers in the 90th percentile of the distribution have greater earnings premiums than other lawyers do, but premiums for lawyers in the 25th and 50th percentiles have increased by the greatest percentage over time.

The relatively high rate of growth in earnings premiums for lawyers with incomes in the lower half of the earnings distribution may be

13. The parameter estimates are consistent but not necessarily efficient (Powell 1986). Chernozhukov and Hong (2002) propose a three-step estimator for censored quantile regression that is likely to produce efficiency gains, but the earnings premiums coefficients obtained here with the simpler estimator are statistically significant at the 1 percent level.

Table 3-5. *Quantile Regression Estimates of Lawyers' Earnings Premiums, Selected Quantiles and Years*[a]

| | Quantile | | | |
| | 0.25 | | 0.50 | |
Year	Earnings premium	Income at percentile	Earnings premium	Income at percentile
1975	0.216	13,200	0.237	20,000
1985	0.301	26,000	0.313	39,000
1995	0.346	40,000	0.333	60,000
2004	0.444	60,000	0.480	100,000
	0.75		0.90	
1975	0.299	31,382	0.407	43,000
1985	0.320	60,000	0.577	96,000
1995	0.365	90,000	0.630	135,000
2004	0.512	150,000	0.710	300,000[b]

Source: Authors' calculations.

a. All coefficient estimates are statistically significant at the 1 percent confidence level and are computed at the sample means of all other explanatory variables.

b. In 2004, 15 percent of lawyers in the sample had incomes at the 90th percentile that were censored; thus, their incomes are reported as the product of the upper limit of reported income in the CPS and the inflator of 1.5. Lawyers' incomes in all other years in the table were not censored at the 90th percentile.

explained by entry restrictions that disproportionately keep out "marginal" would-be lawyers. At the same time, the most highly paid lawyers, such as partners at large law firms, may also benefit from restrictions on entry because their incomes derive in large part from revenues generated by lower-paid associates in their firms. In addition, greater demand for legal work in the federal arena is certainly likely to benefit lawyers at the upper end of the earnings distribution who are employed at mid-size and large firms that are better able to satisfy demand created by government actions. In sum, it is clear that lawyers at all income levels—not just the highest earners—are receiving substantial earnings premiums that have increased over time.

To provide additional understanding of the sources of the earnings premiums, it is useful to assess whether they vary much by firm size. Unfortunately, the CPS only began to report the number of people who work for the respondent's employer in the late 1980s, and it did so only in aggregate firm size (employees) categories of 1–9, 10–24, 25–99, 100–499, and 500+. Unable, as a result, to estimate a quantile regression of earnings based on firm size, we therefore explored various interactions of the firm size category variables with the lawyer occupational dummy and found that its effects did not vary significantly across the firm sizes of 10–24, 25–99, and 100–499, so we report results for those three firm sizes as a single group. The estimated coefficients of interest, all of which are statistically significant at the 1 percent level, are:

	1995	2004
Occupational dummy: firms with 1–9 employees	.22	.36
Occupational dummy: firms with 10–499 employees	.50	.59
Occupational dummy: firms with 500+ employees	.39	.58

The estimates indicate that the premiums earned by lawyers employed at the smallest law firms are lower than the earnings premiums for lawyers employed at larger law firms. Two possible explanations for this finding are that junior lawyers (associates) at very small law firms earn smaller premiums than associates earn at larger, prestigious firms, and that lawyers who are partners at very small firms extract fewer earnings premiums from their associates than partners extract at larger firms.[14] In addition, we cannot discount the possibility that the findings reflect selectivity bias to the extent that lawyers with greater unobserved abilities and skills elect to work at larger law firms.

14. Our finding is broadly consistent with a study by Heinz and others (2005) of members of the Chicago bar. They find that in 1995 solo practitioners accounted for 15 percent of practicing lawyers but only 10 percent of total income, whereas firms with 100 or more lawyers accounted for 25 percent of practicing lawyers and 37 percent of total income. The *Wall Street Journal*, "Legal Heavies Tackle the First-Year Associate Dilemma," December 9, 2009, reports that clients have never liked paying hundreds of thousands of dollars to first- and second-year associates at major law firms. Recently, some in-house counsels have built "no-first-or-second-year" provisions into their arrangements with large law firms. But Peter Kalis, the chair of the law firm K&L Gates, claims that the entry-level associates still have to be paid, so firms raise their rates for senior associates and partners.

We also find that lawyers employed at the largest law firms earned lower earnings premiums in 1995 than did lawyers employed at the mid-size law firms. That difference narrowed considerably in the next decade, however, possibly because the largest firms began to make greater internal efforts to reduce "free riding" by shedding the least productive partners. In the wake of the 2007 recession, those firms may have intensified such efforts.

Robustness Checks

Workers' earnings may also be influenced by certain job characteristics such as annual hours of work and areas of specialization and by unobserved personal attributes related to intellectual ability and skills. The omission of those effects in the preceding analysis could bias the estimates of lawyers' earnings premiums, implying that it would be misleading to conclude that they reflect market inefficiencies. We conduct several tests to explore how those omissions affect our estimates of lawyers' earnings premiums over time.

JOB CHARACTERISTICS. Henderson (2006) reports that average annual billable hours by law firm associates remained remarkably stable between 1985 and 2003 at 1,850, while average annual billable hours by partners rose from 1,538 to 1,703 during this period. The rise in billable hours for partners could be explained by the growth in nonequity partners, who bill hours alongside associates. Lawyers' annual hours of work reported in the CPS, which does not distinguish between partners and associates, rose slightly between 1976 and 2005. Of course, those figures reflect averages and may hide variations in billable hours that are reflected in earnings premiums. We explored this possibility by including CPS survey respondents' hours of work in the earnings equations and reestimating the models. Although one should be cautious about the consistency of the estimated coefficient for hours of work because of endogeneity bias, the inclusion of the hours variable in the earnings equations barely affected the estimates of the occupational dummies for lawyers.

The total annual hours of work is also probably an important factor that contributes to job satisfaction. Although formal measures of other factors that contribute to job satisfaction are difficult to develop, Heinz and others (2005) conclude from surveys that lawyers are as satisfied with their jobs as are people in other professions. Thus, aspects of job satisfaction that are difficult to measure are unlikely to be an important determinant of lawyers' earnings, and their omission unlikely to seriously bias the estimates of the coefficient of the lawyers' occupational dummy.

AREAS OF SPECIALIZATION. Lawyers' earnings may also be affected by their areas of specialization. For example, attorneys who specialize in corporate and antitrust work at large law firms in New York and Washington, D.C., may have greater earnings and possibly greater earning premiums than lawyers who specialize in other fields of law. Unfortunately, the CPS does not indicate lawyers' areas of specialization; thus we take a suggestive approach and use geography as a proxy for areas of specialization. In 2006 average revenue per lawyer at thirty of the nation's largest law firms exceeded $800,000; twenty-four of those firms are located (or headquartered) in New York, Boston, and Washington. To determine if our results are simply reflecting the success of those large law firms and their preeminence in antitrust and corporate work, we estimated the earnings equations on a subsample of workers who were employed in the New York, Boston, and Washington metropolitan statistical areas using tobit and least squares after multiplying censored incomes by 1.5. We found that the estimated coefficients for the lawyers' occupational dummies in this subsample were quite similar to the estimates based on the full sample. Of course, estimates based on subsamples of lawyers by area of specialization would be more persuasive.

ABILITIES. Workers' abilities are likely to affect their earnings; therefore the omission of ability-related variables from the model could bias estimates of the occupational dummy. Unfortunately, ability is difficult to measure, and no explicit measure of it over time is available in the CPS sample. Abrams and Yoon (2007) evaluated the ability of attorneys who were randomly assigned cases in the Clark

County, Nevada, Office of the Public Defender to eliminate the possibility of selection bias in their case assignments. The authors found that attorneys' performance, as measured by the length of a defendant's sentence and incarceration, varied considerably and was well-correlated with their observable characteristics, including the length of tenure on the job, race, and plea bargaining behavior, but was not correlated with the law school they had attended.

Our finding that lawyers' earnings premiums have increased over the past three decades may reflect the rising relative abilities of new entrants into the legal profession. To examine whether the average (intellectual) ability of entrants into the legal profession increased during the period of our analysis, we roughly characterize lawyers' intellectual abilities based on the mean LSAT score and mean grade point average of people admitted to law school and on the percentage of admitted students who had a postgraduate degree. Data provided by the Law School Admissions Council suggest no marked improvement, on average, in the intellectual abilities of people pursuing a career in law during our sample period. Specifically, the mean LSAT scores of admitted students have changed very little from the late 1970s to 2004.[15] The grade point average of people admitted to at least one law school in the United States has barely increased since the late 1970s, rising from 3.25 to 3.34 in 2004. Because this increase does not control for grade inflation, the actual increase in admittants' grade point average is likely to be less.[16] The actual number of admitted students with a postgraduate degree has remained constant at around 6,000,

15. LSAT scores are standardized; thus, a given test taker's LSAT score is compared with other test takers' scores during the same period. But unless the mean intellectual ability of *all* LSAT test takers has changed substantially during our period of analysis, the small change in the mean score of *admitted* students suggests that their ability has changed little over time. If lawyers' ability had changed substantially, the mean scores would have clearly increased.

16. Accounting for grade inflation may erode those observed gains in grade point averages entirely. In a survey of grading practices at eight liberal arts colleges, Sabot and Wakeman-Lin (1991) found that the aggregate grade points awarded in introductory courses increased by roughly 1 percent a year from 1962 to 1985. Meanwhile, the nominal grade point average of people admitted to law school increased 0.09 point from the late 1970s to 2004, only one-

indicating that the share has actually fallen because the number of admitted students has increased.

Although our crude measures have found scant evidence of improvements in lawyers' abilities over the sample period, it is also important to assess whether abilities in the general population have changed. Lawyers' occupational premiums are estimated in comparison with premiums in other occupations including those that require and those that do not require a particular college degree. Thus, if abilities have declined in the general population, the lawyers' occupational dummy may be capturing relative returns to ability.

Since 1974 the General Social Survey, conducted by the National Opinion Research Center at the University of Chicago, has given the Wordsum vocabulary test to a representative sample of American adults. This test has been interpreted by some researchers as a test of ability; it is, in fact, a test of one component of verbal ability, and its findings should be interpreted with caution. In any case, the results of this test indicate that the frequency of correct responses to vocabulary tests of the definitions of easy and hard words remained fairly constant between 1974 and 2000 (Malhotra, Krosnick, and Haertel 2007).

If lawyers' abilities have increased over time (that is, if new lawyers are "better" than existing lawyers), then the wage premium from years of work experience should decrease over time because it is a less important determinant of performance. To test this proposition, we modified our earnings equation by interacting the years of work experience variables with the lawyer occupational dummy (all other variables were specified as before) and reestimated all of the equations. The coefficients for the lawyers' experience variables remained essentially stable over time, a result that is inconsistent with the theory that the innate abilities of new lawyers have been noticeably improving.

Finally, one could argue that if earnings premiums in the legal profession are rising, recent entrants in pursuit of those premiums should have markedly greater ability (as measured by higher LSAT scores and grade point averages) than past entrants possessed. However, some

---

tenth of the implied inflation rate of 1 percent, suggesting a *decrease* in admitted students' "real" grade point average.

highly able people who might have entered the legal profession during the past few decades were likely attracted instead to potentially more lucrative opportunities offered by technology start-ups, investment banks, or venture capital firms, for example.[17] Of course, the recent financial crisis is likely to have temporarily reduced the appeal of those opportunities, but as noted it initially did not dissuade people who are interested in a legal career.

RETURN TO SKILLS. Labor economists have argued that the pay premium for skills has increased in recent years, not because people today have relatively more talent than people did several decades ago, but rather because of changes in pay-setting institutions or skill-biased technical change, that is, a shift in production technology that favors more educated, more able, and more experienced labor over unskilled labor. The pay premium for skills appears to coincide with the rapid diffusion of information and communication technology at workplaces since the 1980s. Hanushek and Woessmann (2007) summarize the evidence of increasing returns to skills, which could also account for the rising earnings premiums that we found for lawyers. Card and DiNardo (2002) do not question the advances in computer-related technology but conclude that the evidence linking rising wage inequality and skill-biased technical change is surprisingly weak. Lemieux (2006) finds little evidence of a pervasive increase in the demand for skill attributable to skill-biased technological change and concludes that any increase in the return to unobserved skills during 1973 to 2003, a period that is aligned with our sample, was concentrated in the 1980s. And Fortin and Lemieux (1997) question the extent of that increase because they find that changes during the 1980s in regulatory policy, the real value of the minimum wage, and deunionization are linked with rising wage inequality.

17. It is also possible that certain individuals who seek high earnings obtain a law degree but go into another line of work without ever practicing law. For example, roughly 40 individuals with law degrees were included in the *Forbes* list of the 400 wealthiest Americans in 2010. However, only one of them, Joe Jamail, referred to as the King of Torts, was a practicing attorney.

Our estimation results provide circumstantial evidence contradicting the view that lawyers' earning premiums reflect returns to skill. Although it is reasonable to believe that lawyers have enhanced their skills by being able to use advances in information technology to conduct legal research more effectively and to communicate with clients, our findings, shown in table 3-4, indicate that the growth in lawyers' earning premiums was not affected by changes over time in capital utilization and output; such changes are likely to be associated with advances in information technology. Thus, if lawyers' earning premiums are truly capturing returns to skill-biased technical change, they are capturing only the component of technical change that is not associated with greater capital utilization and output. We are not able to identify that component.

We also note the highly unlikely probability that an important omitted measure of skills that would affect lawyers' earnings premiums would not also affect the earnings premiums in other occupations, such as medicine and engineering, whose members possess above-average skills. A close look at the estimated earnings premiums for all the occupations in table 3-3 indicates that most of them have been stable over time.[18] Three notable exceptions are dentists, pharmacists, and economists, all of whose earnings premiums have increased since 1995. As noted, the increase in dentists' earnings premiums is consistent with the decline in the supply of dental school graduates attributable to dental school closings during the latter part of our sample. The increase in earnings premiums for pharmacists and economists appears to be explained by certain changes affecting market conditions in those professions that began in the past few decades.

The first degree in pharmacy was a four-year bachelor of science in pharmacy. In 1990 the American Association of Colleges of Pharmacy mandated that a doctorate in pharmacy, or PharmD, would be the new first degree, requiring at least six years of study and the passing of a state board of pharmacy's licensure examination. Additional exams must then be passed to actually become a practicing pharma-

18. This conclusion also holds for the additional occupational earnings premiums that were estimated in our sensitivity analysis discussed previously.

cist. As of 2000 all pharmacy schools in the United States had discontinued the four-year degree in pharmacy and offered only the six-year degree. According to the Pharmacy College Application Service, admission to a pharmacy school is difficult; roughly two-thirds of people who apply are not admitted to any school. Thus, the supply of pharmacists has become much more constrained during a period of growing demand for health services.

Siegfried and Stock (2006) point out that the number of U.S. citizens earning a doctorate in economics has been declining for the past few decades, which could reflect a stricter certification constraint for U.S. citizens that is attributable to the growing technical difficulty of economics doctoral programs or to an increase in (strong) international students. But economists are not subject to occupational licensing; thus, some other factor is likely to explain the recent increase in their earnings premiums. Beginning in the 1980s a larger share of new economics doctorates found employment in the private sector instead of in academia. For example, the Survey of Earned Doctorates, conducted by the National Opinion Research Center at the University of Chicago, indicated that during 1975–79 roughly 10 percent of new PhDs in economics who were employed and were U.S. citizens or permanent residents worked in industry instead of in academia. Since 1995 that figure has been as high as 25 percent, and the growth in private sector employment would undoubtedly be higher if the survey included non-U.S. citizens. As Mandel (1999) observed, the growth of economic consulting firms, especially those that provide litigation support, has provided an alternative—and often more financially rewarding—career path for young PhD economists and has helped boost academic economists' absolute and relative salaries.[19] By 1991 economists had become the most common type of expert witness in federal civil trials (Krafka and others 2002). Thus it appears that the growing alliance

19. For example, Ehrenberg, McGraw, and Mrdjenovic (2006) report that, for a large sample of colleges and universities, the average salary of full professors in economics relative to the average salary of full professors in English language and literature rose from 114 percent in 1985–86 to 128 percent in 2001–02. The differential for assistant professors grew during this period from 133 percent to 149 percent.

between the economics profession and the legal profession has helped economists gain greater earnings premiums.[20] Kleiner (2006) presents evidence consistent with this conclusion; his comparison of their parameter estimates yields a difference of only 0.048.

AN EMPIRICAL EXPLORATION OF BIAS. We use the Panel Study of Income Dynamics (PSID) to investigate empirically whether unobserved worker characteristics including skills are biasing our estimates of the coefficients of lawyers' occupational dummy. In contrast to the CPS, the PSID is a longitudinal study of a representative sample of U.S. households that does not censor earnings. The sample grew from 4,800 households in 1968 to 7,000 households in 2001. We constructed a sample of the data containing information that corresponds as closely as possible to the CPS sample. Because of the limited availability of variables in the earlier years and a marked disruption of the study in the mid-1990s, which has raised concerns about the reliability of the data following the disruption, our PSID sample period runs from 1981 to 1992. We included households that contributed data for this entire period as well as households that joined the panel at some point during this period; the head of household is the primary information source.

Compared with the CPS sample, the strength of the PSID sample is that it contains repeated observations for the same individuals over time, which enables us to pool the data to explore whether estimated occupational choice coefficients are biased by changes in unobserved characteristics over time. Unfortunately, we are unable to include as many occupational dummies as we do in the CPS sample because of the smaller sample size. However, we did have a sufficient number of lawyers in the sample (as many as 30 in any given year and roughly 250 observations in total) to obtain a precise estimate of their occupational dummy. The final specification of the head of household's annual earnings included years of work experience; race; gender; age; and dummies for education, occupation, year, and geographical region.

---

20. The recent growth in economists' earnings premiums might also reflect increasing consulting and employment opportunities in the financial industry.

As noted, we are not able to address the issue of bias in our estimates of lawyers' occupational premiums by improving the specification or estimation of the earnings equation. As a next best approach, we accept the possibility of bias and use a procedure developed by Altonji, Elder, and Taber (2005) to characterize the extent of the bias that may be attributable to unobserved skills. The authors attribute the problem to sample selectivity. In our case, the estimate of the lawyer occupational dummy variable may be biased because individuals who choose to become lawyers do so because they have certain unobserved characteristics, including skills, which are not widely shared by individuals who choose to work in other occupations. As a robustness check, Altonji, Elder, and Taber suggest that the extent of this bias may be compared with the extent that *observed* individual characteristics explain occupational choices.

Formally, we consider the wage equation (suppressing time subscripts for simplicity)

$$w_i = X_i'\beta + \gamma D_i + \varepsilon_i, \tag{3-2}$$

where w_i is individual i's wage, X_i' is a vector of individual i's observed exogenous characteristics, β is a vector of parameters; D_i is an endogenous occupational dummy variable (equal to 1 if individual i is a lawyer, and 0 otherwise); γ is the coefficient of the occupational dummy; and ε_i is an error term consisting of unobserved determinants of w_i including skills.

Least squares (OLS) estimates of lawyers' earnings premiums ($\hat{\gamma}$) are unbiased if the component of earnings that is related to unobserved individual characteristics has no relationship with the choice of an individual to become a lawyer (that is, the lawyer dummy). The formal condition, which is unlikely to be completely satisfied in our context, is $\text{cov}(D^*, \varepsilon) = 0$ where D^* is the component of the effect of occupational choice on wages that is orthogonal to the other variables X. But if an individual's choice to become a lawyer is related to the component of earnings reflecting the individual's unobserved characteristics in the same way as it is related to the individual's observed characteristics, namely,

$$\text{cov}\big(D,\varepsilon\big)=\text{cov}\big(X'\beta,D\big), \qquad\qquad (3\text{-}3)$$

then we can measure the magnitude of the bias from individuals who select their occupation based on unobserved characteristics relative to selecting their occupation based on observed characteristics. Given the binary specification of D_p, Altonji, Elder, and Taber show that equation 3-3 is equivalent to

$$\frac{E\big(\varepsilon|D=1\big)-E\big(\varepsilon|D=0\big)}{Var\big(\varepsilon\big)}=\frac{E\big(X'\beta|D=1\big)-E\big(X'\beta|D=0\big)}{Var\big(X'\beta\big)}. \qquad (3\text{-}4)$$

To determine the strength of the evidence in favor of occupational earnings premiums unrelated to unobserved skills (that is, $\gamma > 0$), we consider how large the ratio on the left-hand-side of equation 3-4 would have to be to account fully for the estimated $\hat{\gamma}$ under the null hypothesis that $\gamma = 0$. In other words, the case for the existence of lawyers' earnings premiums unrelated to unobserved skills is strengthened the more that selection on unobserved variables is required to exceed selection on observed variables. If the choice to become a lawyer were fully explained by observed worker characteristics, an omitted variable (for example, occupational skill) biasing the coefficient $\hat{\gamma}$ would not exist.

Let ε^D be the residual of a first-stage probit regression of the (assumed) endogenous occupational dummy variable D on the observed variables X. Following Altonji, Elder, and Taber, we approximate the bias from a probit estimation in a similar manner as the bias in an OLS estimation. The expression for the approximate bias in $\hat{\gamma}$ from OLS estimation of equation 3-2 is

$$\text{plim}\hat{\gamma}\approx\gamma+\left(\frac{Cov\big(\varepsilon^D,\varepsilon\big)}{Var\big(\varepsilon^D\big)}\right). \qquad\qquad (3\text{-}5)$$

In the case where D is binary, equation 3-5 can be rewritten as

$$\text{plim}\hat{\gamma}\approx\gamma+\frac{Var\big(D\big)}{Var\big(\varepsilon^D\big)}\big(E\big(\varepsilon|D=1\big)-E\big(\varepsilon|D=0\big)\big). \qquad (3\text{-}6)$$

Given equation 3-6 and the null hypothesis that $\gamma = 0$, the amount of selection bias induced by unobservable characteristics on an individual's occupational choice would have to be

$$\frac{\hat{\gamma}}{\left(Var(D)/Var(\varepsilon^D)\right)\left(E(\varepsilon|D=1)-E(\varepsilon|D=0)\right)} \tag{3-7}$$

times larger than the amount of selection from observed characteristics to account fully for a finding of occupational earnings premiums unrelated to unobserved skills. While this ratio has no formal critical value, Altonji, Elder, and Taber cautiously offer a rule of thumb that occupational earnings premiums are likely to exist if this ratio exceeds one. That is, for occupational earnings premiums to be completely dismissed as an artifact of selection bias, unobserved worker attributes must play a larger role in determining earnings than do observed worker attributes—an unlikely occurrence in our case given the broad set of worker characteristics that make up X.

Table 3-6 presents estimation results of an earnings equation based on our PSID sample. Generally, the estimated coefficients are aligned with our previous estimates based on the CPS sample: earnings are positively related to a college education and work experience, albeit at a decreasing rate; earnings are lower for females, nonwhites, and the elderly; and doctors' earnings premiums tend to be larger than lawyers' earnings premiums.

Of particular importance to our investigation is the estimate of the occupational dummy variable for lawyers, $\hat{\gamma}$; it is positive and statistically significant. It is also somewhat larger than the estimated coefficients for the lawyer dummy based on the CPS sample, possibly because annual wages are not censored.[21]

---

21. We explored whether the lawyers' occupational dummy may have been larger because we were not able to include as many occupational dummies in the specification as we could using the CPS data. We found that adding additional occupational dummies slightly reduced the occupational dummy for lawyers but that it remained within one standard deviation of the current estimate.

Table 3-6. *Estimates of Earnings Based on a Longitudinal Sample, 1981–92*[a]

Independent variable	Generalized least squares coefficient
Education dummy (1 if college completed; 0 otherwise)	0.134
	(0.010)
Years of work experience	0.088
	(0.002)
Years of work experience squared	–0.002
	(0.00004)
Race dummy (1 if non–white, 0 if white)	–0.337
	(0.010)
Gender dummy (1 if female, 0 if male)	–0.516
	(0.012)
Age of head of household	–0.017
	(0.001)
Lawyer dummy (1 if individual is lawyer, 0 otherwise)	0.849
	(0.059)
Doctor dummy (1 if individual is doctor, 0 otherwise)	1.232
	(0.093)
Year dummies included	Yes
Regional dummies included	Yes
Number of observations	43,504
Number of individuals	9,774
R^2	0.21

Source: Authors' calculations.

a. Dependent variable: Natural log of year's wages (before deductions) from the head of household's primary job; all monetary values in real 2005 dollars. Heteroskedastic robust standard errors in parentheses.

The estimate of $\hat{\gamma}$ presented in table 3-6 is used in the numerator of the expression in equation 3-7. We use the data in the PSID sample to calculate $Var\,(D)$ and obtain $Var\,(\varepsilon^D)$ from a probit estimation of the occupation dummy D on the explanatory variables in the model. Finally, we use the parameter estimates in table 3-6 to calculate the conditional expectations of ε. Putting all of the estimates together, we find that selection into the legal profession based on unobserved individual characteristics must be 1.38 times larger than selection based on observed individual characteristics if the estimate of earnings premiums to lawyers is to be fully explained by estimation bias. This relative "explanatory power" of unobserved characteristics is extremely unlikely given that we observe several important determinants of occupational choice, thus providing support for the conclusion that we are in fact identifying positive occupational earnings premiums to lawyers.

Summary

We earlier estimated that the United States is spending $170 billion a year on lawyers (in 2005 dollars), with lawyers at private firms accounting for roughly 77 percent of the expenditures. In this chapter, we estimated earnings equations to quantify the share of those expenditures that can be characterized as occupational earnings premiums. Based on those estimates, we find that by 2004 lawyers' earnings premiums amounted to $64 billion—or an eye-popping $71,000 per practicing lawyer—and that those premiums were widely shared among the legal profession.

We have conducted several formal and informal tests to explore whether our estimates of earnings premiums reflect market inefficiencies or are instead capturing particular job characteristics or selectivity into the legal profession that reflect omitted measures of ability and skills. We have found that:

—lawyers' earnings premiums were not affected by the number of annual hours worked;

—lawyers' earnings premiums were not affected by area of specialization as proxied by geographical place of work;

—lawyers' earnings premiums were not likely to be explained by other job characteristics that contribute to job satisfaction;

—the average ability of lawyers has not changed much during the sample period, according to LSAT scores and grade point averages;

—the effect of experience on lawyers' earnings has remained constant over time, suggesting that the ability of new lawyers has not increased over time;

—the temporal pattern of lawyers' estimated earnings premiums either differs from or is similar to the temporal pattern of estimated earnings premiums in other occupations in ways that are consistent with the effect of various policies on the supply and demand for those occupations rather than on the effect of an unobserved measure of skills;

—the extent to which our estimates of earnings premiums are biased because of the omission of unobserved skills is likely to be small, based on a procedure developed by Altonji, Elder, and Taber (2005).

In their totality and in combination with other evidence in the literature that we presented, those findings constitute strong support for the argument that lawyers are, in fact, earning premiums that reflect market inefficiencies. But to reinforce that conclusion, we must document empirically the factors that explain lawyers' earnings premiums and explain why those factors reflect inefficient market forces on lawyers' earnings.

CHAPTER FOUR

Sources of Lawyers' Earnings Premiums

Katz and Summers (1989) concluded that workers in some industries appear to receive wage premiums that could not be explained by differences in skills or in working conditions. The efficiency wage literature suggests that wage premiums persist because firms may find that the gain in profits from reducing wages may be offset by lower productivity. This argument, however, does not seem to explain lawyers' earnings premiums because law partners share ownership of their firm—that is, their pay derives from dividing up the firm's profits—and, as noted, Rebitzer and Taylor (1995) concluded that associates are not paid efficiency wages. In this chapter, we focus on the external forces that we as economists would expect to drive lawyers' earnings premiums. We begin by investigating whether the licensure requirements have helped lawyers to become an effective interest group that is able to overcome free riding and benefit from certain government policies. We then demonstrate the significant role that various government policies have had in increasing lawyers' earnings premiums over time.

The Licensing Constraint and Free Riding

All successful political interest groups must be represented by an effective lobbying organization, and lawyers are no exception. American Bar Association regulations and state laws restrict membership in the legal profession, which has the effect of preventing free riding (Becker 1983).[1] If entry were not restricted, we would expect that additional lawyers—that is, an increase in supply—would eventually erode any earnings premiums that are unrelated to efficient market forces. If the ABA, with the help of state laws, is constraining the growth of lawyers to maintain or increase their earnings premiums, it should allow entry only up to the point that its members' incomes are maximized, accounting for the effect of additional members on the legal profession's ability to influence public policy and increase premiums. In contrast, if the ABA is unable to prevent entry into the legal profession from growing beyond this level, some new entrants may dissipate earnings premiums.

We explore the effect of the (constrained) supply of lawyers on lawyers' earnings premiums by first assuming that entry restrictions allow supply to be treated as an exogenous determinant of the premiums. This is a plausible assumption because we have carefully documented that the supply of lawyers is determined by an outside agency (the ABA) and the state governments rather than by market forces that could be affecting premiums through other channels. We then test the effectiveness of the ABA constraint on the supply of lawyers by running a regression for the period 1975–2004 of lawyers' earnings premiums (as measured previously and reported in the first column of table 3-4 in chapter 3), on the total number of lawyers (in hundreds of thousands) in the United States, given in figure 2-2 in chapter 2. We obtain a coefficient of 0.047 with a standard error of 0.010 ($R^2 = 0.39$).[2] Thus the marginal lawyer has a *positive* effect on earnings pre-

1. The American Bar Association does have its critics within the legal profession who think it should do even more to limit the supply of lawyers. For example, Mark Greenbaum, "No More Room at the Bench," *Los Angeles Times*, January 8, 2010, claims that the ABA has not been tough enough in its accreditation of new law schools to stem the flow of lawyers in a "saturated marketplace." Greenbaum calls for federal action to stop this flow or for the U.S. Department of Education to strip the ABA of its accreditor status and give the authority to a different organization that is free of conflicts of interest. Greenbaum does not identify the ABA's conflicts of interest.

2. We corrected for serial correlation in the regression. When we lagged the number of lawyers one year and estimated earnings premiums, the coefficient was 0.044 with a standard error of 0.010 ($R^2 = 0.40$).

miums, and this effect is precisely estimated. In other words, the licensing constraint is enabling lawyers to behave as an effective interest group that receives earnings premiums and is sufficiently tight to prevent an additional entrant, who may be a free rider, from reducing average premiums.

We doubt that the number of lawyers per se simply reflects individuals' selection into the profession, but the possibility of selectivity bias can be addressed in this simple regression by using the number of accredited law schools (as given in figure 2-1, in chapter 2) as an instrument for the number of lawyers. The number of accredited law schools is exogenously determined by the American Bar Association and is well correlated with the number of lawyers, but it is not driven by the demand for law spaces, which might be affected by earnings premiums. In fact, Law School Admission Council data indicate that the numbers of applicants and applications to law schools have risen and fallen during the past two decades, while the number of law schools has slowly increased. When we estimate the effect of the number of lawyers on lawyers' earnings premiums using the number of law schools as an instrument for the number of lawyers, the coefficient obtained by instrumental variables estimation is 0.048 with a standard error of 0.012 ($R^2 = 0.31$), which is virtually the same as our previous ordinary least squares estimate and is consistent with our interpretation that occupational licensing is enabling lawyers to behave as an effective interest group.[3] Other aspects of lawyers' interest group behavior are discussed in chapter 5.

The Effect of Government Policies

The effect of occupational licensing on lawyers' earnings is magnified by government policies that generate massive demand for legal services by private firms and government agencies while the supply of lawyers remains constrained. We document the point empirically by showing

3. We corrected for serial correlation in the regression. When we lagged the number of lawyers one year and estimated earnings premiums by instrumental variables, the coefficient was 0.052 with a standard error of 0.013 ($R^2 = 0.37$).

that a representative set of government policies has contributed to the growth in lawyers' earnings premiums. Of course, this increase may be a cost that is offset by the implementation of policies that enhance social welfare and require more legal services. Thus we report the available scholarly empirical assessments of those policies that have the greatest effect on lawyers' premiums. Our general finding is that those policies provide some benefits to society, but they also generate costs. On net, the most important of those policies associated with increasing lawyers' earnings premiums appear to have an adverse effect on social welfare; thus, it would be desirable to curtail them, thereby reducing lawyers' premiums. Accordingly, lawyers have an incentive to support those inefficient policies to maintain their premiums. We discuss later how the legal profession actually provides such support.

The following policies are included in our empirical analysis:

—economic regulations intended to curb market power

—social regulations designed to address externalities such as pollution

—financial regulations to prevent information asymmetries from undermining the efficiency of securities markets

—patent protection for intellectual property

—liability rules to help settle claims of civil wrongs

—enforcement of criminal laws to protect the public

—the establishment of legal guidelines to facilitate commercial and residential property transactions

We estimate a time-series regression of the impacts of government policies on our estimates of lawyers' annual earnings premiums at the national level. The unit of observation is appropriate because it is largely the effect of changes in federal government policy over time on lawyers' earnings premiums that we are concerned with and because our independent variables incorporate federal, state, and even local legal matters that are aggregated to the national level.

We are not aware of data that would enable us to divide law firm revenues between matters involving state and local issues and those involving federal issues, but there are strong indications that a large share of the law profession's revenues derives from issues or requirements that are controlled or resolved in Washington, not in the states.

Law firms that specialize in serving business clients account for a substantial share of revenues;[4] a large share of legal services activity originates in four jurisdictions, the District of Columbia, California, Illinois, and New York, undoubtedly because the three states are home to a large share of the major corporations in the United States that require legal work to comply with federal regulations, pay federal taxes, and the like; a substantial share of individuals' legal services costs, such as complying with federal income and estate taxes, are attributable to federal policies; and even some of the legal services involving state and local government activities, such as highway construction, environmental control, and education, are driven by federal policies.

We specify the base case estimates of lawyers' earnings premiums from 1975 to 2004 (shown in the first column of table 3-4) as the dependent variable.[5] We expect that the government policies in our model contribute to the (rising) demand for lawyers; thus we do not include the number of lawyers in the specification because we do not wish to hold their supply constant. Furthermore, because the earnings premiums are not measured as total dollars, we do not need to standardize them by the size of the legal services industry. Finally, as noted, capital utilization and output do not appear to increase the growth in premiums, but it is useful to control for real gross domestic product (GDP) per worker as a broad measure of the prevailing economic climate.[6]

Based on previous research, we specify the policy variables as follows. Because economic and social regulations are enforced by agencies with regulatory responsibilities, Winston and Crandall (1994)

4. According to *Legal Services: 2002*, U.S. Census Bureau, 2002 Economic Census, table 3, firms, not individual lawyers, account for the majority of the revenues in legal services, and such firms derive more than 80 percent of their revenues from businesses.

5. Because the dependent variable is estimated, it contains measurement error. However, it is unlikely that such error would be systematically related to any of the explanatory variables in the model, so the parameter estimates should be consistent.

6. Real GDP was obtained from the Office of Management and Budget fiscal year 2006 historical tables, and the civilian labor force was obtained from the Bureau of Labor Statistics.

suggest that federal civilian agency employment (excluding military and post office employees) broadly captures the presence and intensity of government regulation. That is, stronger enforcement of existing regulations or new regulations invariably leads to an increase in federal agency employment.[7] As Jaffe and Lerner (2004) indicate, a standard measure of intellectual property protection is the number of patent awards.[8] Following Litan and Winston (1988) and Viscusi (1991), we model the effect of varying liability rules with an annual measure of the real costs of the tort system.[9] We also include data on the Standard & Poor's 500 Equity Index to control for corporate transactions (acquisitions rise with increases in stock market prices), on the value of residential home sales to control for residential property transactions, and on violent crimes committed and reported to control for criminal law enforcement.[10]

Preliminary estimations indicated that home sales and violent crimes had statistically insignificant effects on premiums. We speculate that the

7. Data on the number of federal civilian agency employees were obtained from the Office of Management and Budget fiscal year 2006 historical tables. Other measures of regulatory activity we tried were the number of pages published annually in the *Federal Register*; federal, state, and local government employment (absolute and per capita); and federal government expenditures. Those measures are less precise for our purposes than is federal civilian agency employment, and they produced worse statistical fits.

8. The number of patents awarded was obtained from Jaffe and Lerner (2004). Other measures of intellectual property protection we tried were the number of patent applications and number of patent lawsuits filed. But those measures are less precise for our purposes than is the number of patents awarded, and they produced worse statistical fits.

9. The real costs of the tort system including payouts, payments to lawyers, and insurance costs were obtained from Towers Perrin, Tillinghast's *U.S. Tort Costs and Cross-Border Perspectives: 2005 Update*. We are not aware of alternative sources for the cost for the tort system.

10. The Standard and Poor's 500 index was obtained from Yahoo! Finance. Other less satisfactory corporate-related measures we tried were the number of initial public offerings and mergers and acquisitions filings with the Federal Trade Commission as required by the Hart-Scott-Rodino Act. Home sales and mean prices were obtained from the Department of Housing and Urban Development, "U.S. Housing Market Conditions." Crimes committed and reported were obtained from the U.S. Department of Justice, Bureau of Justice Statistics.

result for home sales reflects the growing use of lower-cost professionals such as real estate brokers and title search companies to perform tasks that may have been performed by lawyers in an earlier era, while the result for law enforcement reflects the fact that many defendants in cases involving violent crimes are represented by a public defender, whose pay on a per client basis has decelerated since 1980 (Hoffman, Rubin, and Shepherd 2005).[11] Finally, we also specified a dummy variable to capture the 1986 federal tax reform, which may have initially generated more work for lawyers but then, after the transition was completed, may have reduced their work by simplifying the tax code. We found the dummy (either by itself or interacted with a trend) had an insignificant effect on lawyers' earnings premiums.

Estimation results for the core policies are presented in table 4-1.[12] Federal nondefense government agency employment, the real annual costs of the tort system, and the annual number of patent awards are associated with increased lawyers' earnings premiums, and the effects are statistically significant. An increase in the S&P 500 index is also associated with an increase in lawyers' earnings premiums, but the statistical reliability of this finding is questionable. Finally, a broad increase in economic activity, as measured by GDP per worker, reduces lawyers' earnings premiums (which can be thought of, after all, as a relative wage premium). This finding is consistent with the prevailing view in the legal profession—at least until recently—that litigation practice is countercyclical.[13] Note that those variables that we have found to contribute to lawyers' earnings premiums are held constant. Thus, we interpret our findings as evidence that lawyers' earnings pre-

11. Figures from the Bureau of Justice Statistics show that 82 percent of federal felony defendants in the seventy-five most populous counties were represented by public defenders in 1996. The figure for all federal felony defendants is 66 percent in 1998 (www.ojp.usdoj.gov/bjs/id.htm).

12. After correcting for serial correlation of the error terms, we did not find that a time trend had a statistically significant effect.

13. In the wake of the financial crisis, a record number of discrimination charges were filed against employers in fiscal year 2010, a phenomenon that has provided more work for lawyers. Other "countercyclical" practices include bankruptcy, securities work, and financial markets regulation.

Table 4-1. *Coefficient Estimates for Determinants of Earnings Premiums of Selected Professions*[a]

Variable	Lawyers	Physicians	Dentists	Economists
Log federal agency employees	0.7209	0.1073	0.9539	0.7733
	(0.1908)	(0.1959)	(0.4417)	(0.2311)
Log real costs of torts	0.1898	−0.0514	−0.2615	0.4144
	(0.0452)	(0.0465)	(0.1078)	(0.1907)
Log number of patents awarded	0.2142	0.1873	0.0138	0.2398
	(0.0812)	(0.0818)	(0.1554)	(0.1842)
Change in real S&P 500 Index	0.00009	−0.0002	−0.0001	0.0002
	(0.00007)	(0.0001)	(0.0001)	(0.0001)
Log real GDP per worker	−0.5477	−0.0985	0.8829	−0.8157
	(0.2747)	(0.2775)	(0.5454)	(0.5490)
Constant	−7.0842	−1.7098	−21.3632	−6.3343
	(3.2046)	(3.2734)	(7.1771)	(5.6825)
Number of observations	30	30	30	20[b]
Adjusted R^2	0.85	0.67	0.36	0.79
Durbin-Watson statistic	2.25	2.06	1.85	2.35

Source: Authors' calculations.
a. Prais-Winsten AR(1) standard errors in parentheses.
b. The sample for economists covers the period 1985 to 2004.

miums relative to earnings in other occupations are not spurred by the general, overall growth of the economy but are in fact driven by specific changes in government policy.[14]

For comparative purposes, the second and third columns of the table show that the policies that significantly increase lawyers' earnings premiums do not tend to increase physicians' and dentists' earnings premiums significantly. As expected, physicians' and, to a larger extent, dentists' earnings premiums are reduced by tort suits. Greater regulatory enforcement, as reflected by the number of agency employees, increase dentists' earnings premiums, possibly because regulations such as occu-

14. We also found that the magnitude and statistical significance of the coefficients for federal employment, tort costs, and patents were not affected much when we specified the dependent variable as lawyers' earnings premiums based on the earnings equations that included output per worker and the capital-labor ratio.

pational health and safety requirements create entry barriers by increasing the costs of setting up a practice and thus limiting competition, while physicians' earnings premiums are raised by an increase in patents—possibly because they are associated with inventions making new, higher-cost treatments possible, which complement physicians' activity. The additional finding that a higher S&P 500 index reduces physicians' and, to a lesser extent, dentists' earnings premiums is consistent with the positive relationship between health and income (Hahn, Lutter, and Viscusi 2000); this effect is not reliably captured by GDP per worker.

Finally, we suggested that the growth in economists' earnings premiums could be attributed to economists' growing interactions with the legal profession. Accordingly, we would expect that economists' premiums could be explained to some extent by the same policies that have contributed to lawyers' premiums. We found this to be the case when we estimated the determinants of economists' earnings premiums for a recent subperiod of our sample, 1985 to 2004, during which time the share of new PhDs in economics who took a job in private industry was steadily growing. The estimated coefficients were much weaker and less significant when we estimated the determinants of economists' earnings premiums over the entire sample period. As shown in the last column of table 4-1, greater regulatory enforcement and the growth of tort suits have a positive and statistically significant effect on economists' earnings premiums, while the effect of patents, although positive, has low statistical reliability. In sum, lawyers and, in recent years, economists appear to have benefited substantially from a broad range of federal policies.

We also investigated the possibility of identifying the effects of federal government policies on lawyers' earnings premiums across states but doing so was difficult for the policies of interest. Patents are filed in Washington, D.C., and challenged or defended in federal courts around the country, and data on employment in regulatory functions and for alternative measures of federal regulatory activity are not available at the state level.

THE WELFARE EFFECTS OF POLICIES THAT INCREASE LAWYERS' PREMIUMS. The positive effects of economic regulations, the liability system, and patents on lawyers' earnings premiums capture inefficient market forces on lawyers' earnings because the empirical evidence indicates that each of those policies has failed to improve social welfare. Winston (2006) synthesized the available evidence on the welfare effects of economic and social regulation including antitrust policy; agricultural subsidies; tariffs and quotas; information policies encompassing advertising, disclosure, product labeling, and product and workplace standards; and policies to correct externalities including airplane noise, air and water pollution, drinking and smoking, and vehicle accidents. Some policies, such as antitrust and information polices, have produced very few documented benefits to consumers, while others, such as some water and emissions pollution policies, have generated large social benefits that have been offset by large social costs. This is not to say that every regulatory policy has been estimated to be socially undesirable, but it is striking that the scholarly evidence has generally failed to identify regulations that have produced significant social gains.[15]

Regarding the liability system, several studies (for example, Huber and Litan 1991) have documented its extensive costs as reflected in higher product prices, the withdrawal of certain products and services from the market, and less innovation. The reduction in injuries and deaths that can be attributed to the system has not been well documented, leading two distinguished law and economics scholars, Polinsky and Shavell (2010b), to suggest that product liability suits likely contribute very little to economic welfare because markets and, to

---

15. President Barack Obama, "Toward a 21st-Century Regulatory System," *Wall Street Journal*, January, 18, 2011, has indicated the importance of carefully assessing existing federal regulations to determine which ones should be eliminated. In addition, the U.S. General Accountability Office, *Opportunities to Reduce Potential Duplication in Government Programs, Save Tax Dollars, and Enhance Revenue*, GAO-11-318SP (March 2011), indicated that another problem with federal regulation is the widespread duplication of agency oversight. GAO concluded that reducing or eliminating duplication and overlap could save billions of tax dollars annually and help agencies be more effective.

some extent, regulators provide sufficient deterrence for manufacturers to offer unsafe products.[16]

Finally, Winston (2006) summarizes the literature that assesses the patent system and concludes that in addition to conferring a monopoly position on an inventor, the current patent system has stymied research and development in several industries and in all likelihood has not provided much incentive for firms to invest in it. Jaffe and Lerner (2004) have argued that there was no empirical justification for the 1982 Federal Courts Improvement Act, which increased the transactions costs of the patent system by shifting patent adjudications to the newly created Federal Circuit, increasing patent applications and awards, and resulting in more patent lawsuits and greater demand for lawyers. Bessen and Meurer (2007) estimate that the real annual private costs of patent litigation (in 1992 dollars), including payments to lawyers, disruption of business operations, greater bankruptcy risks, and animosity between firms that threatens cooperative development, increased from $2 billion in the mid-1980s to $16 billion in 1999. (The costs as a share of annual aggregate R&D more than tripled during the period.)

APPROXIMATING THE EFFECTS OF POLICY CHANGES. What would lawyers' earnings premiums be under counterfactual policy scenarios that try to improve welfare by reducing the costs of regulatory, liability, and patent policies? Of course, we have no way of knowing precisely how such policy changes would evolve, or what sort of inter-

16. Goldberg and Zipursky (2010), in a comment on Polinsky and Shavell (2010b), question the empirical evidence on this point. They also stress that tort liability suits transfer wealth to victims, improving their welfare—a transfer that markets and regulators do not generate. Polinsky and Shavell (2010a) respond by asserting that any benefit from product liability litigation is incremental to the benefits provided by market responses and regulation. They conclude that the burden is therefore on Goldberg and Zipursky to provide empirical evidence that this incremental benefit outweighs the huge cost from using the tort liability system. Polinsky and Shavell also point out that the value of transfers to consumers may be low relative to the cost of providing them; after all, few consumers buy insurance against faulty products or adverse outcomes from using those products.

actions between those and other policies may have contributed to the growth in lawyers' earnings premiums. We perform the analysis by using the estimated coefficients from the time series model in table 4-1 and by constructing several alternative policy landscapes.

First, federal employment increases lawyers' earnings premiums through government regulatory actions that increase the demand for lawyers. Winston and Crandall (1994) estimated that the number of employees of the agencies or the divisions of Executive Branch departments who are directly involved in regulation, including economic and social regulatory activities, was slightly less than 100,000 in 1992. Warren (2000) subsequently estimated that this figure had risen to 130,000 by 2000. To reduce the cost of regulations, we therefore simulate the effect on lawyers' earnings premiums of a phased-in linear annual reduction of federal nondefense employment so that 100,000 employees are terminated by the end of our sample period, which still leaves more than 30,000 employees who are directly involved in regulation.[17]

Second, from 1975 to 2004 real tort costs increased 4.5 percent a year, or roughly 1.5 times the average growth in real GDP. Several policies could be implemented to reduce the cost of the tort system, such as imposing limitations on class-action suits, capping punitive damages, imposing the British rule of "loser pays," or possibly limiting the use of contingency contracts by lawyers. In addition, the level of safety in a society generally improves with rising income (Wildavsky 1988). Thus it is unlikely that the cost of the tort system should rise more rapidly than a broad measure of income, GDP, which is causing society to become safer. We therefore simulate the effect on lawyers' earnings premiums of the adoption by federal or state governments of one or more policies that would keep real tort costs growing at the same rate as real GDP from 1975 to 2004, namely, 3 percent a year.

---

17. We are assuming that the reduction in employees would come from those who are directly involved in regulation and that the vast majority of federal civilian employees who are indirectly involved in regulation would still be employed by the government.

Finally, as noted, the 1982 Federal Courts Improvement Act significantly increased the transactions costs of the patent system. The effect of the new court's decisions was not felt immediately, but the rise in patent litigation appears to have begun in 1986. Between 1986 and 2004 patent awards increased at a rate of 5 percent a year after exhibiting virtually no growth during the previous eleven years. It is reasonable to expect that the revolution in information technology would cause the rate of patenting during 1986–2004 to increase over the rate observed during 1975–86, but in the absence of the change in judicial oversight, the increase would plausibly be aligned with the growth in GDP.[18] We therefore assume that real annual patent awards increased 3 percent a year after 1986.

To analyze the effects of those policy scenarios, we first used our estimated lawyers' earnings premiums equation in table 4-1 and predicted lawyer premiums from 1975 through 2004 under historical conditions; that is, not incorporating our hypothetical policy changes. We then adjusted the regulatory, liability, and patent policy variables based on the preceding assumptions and obtained new, counterfactual predictions of lawyers' earnings premiums. As shown in table 4-2, lawyers' earnings premiums are profoundly affected by the policy scenarios we have outlined. Under each scenario, lawyers' earnings premiums decline some 6 to 8 percentage points by 2004. Collectively, our simulated policy changes forestall much of the growth in lawyers' premiums that has occurred since the mid-1970s, reducing lawyers' average annual earnings roughly $36,000 by 2004. Of course, scenarios that assume less dramatic rollbacks in government policy—for example, a phased-in reduction in federal regulatory employment of 50,000 instead of 100,000—would result in commensurately smaller reductions in lawyers' premiums. To be fair, caution is warranted when sim-

18. The European Commission reports that patent awards rose rapidly in the United States while remaining relatively constant in the European Union in the early 1990s. Clearly, the high-tech revolution affected both continents, but it induced much more patent activity in the United States. See EU Commission, RTD Info, "Strengths and Weaknesses of European S&T," 1997 (http://ec.europa.eu/research/rtdinf20/en/st.html).

Table 4-2. *Estimated Effects of Government Policy Initiatives on Lawyers' Earnings Premiums, 1975–2004*

Year	Predicted premium from lawyers' premium equation assuming no policy changes[a]	Estimated premium with tort cost growth reduced to 3% a year	Estimated premium with patent award growth reduced to 3% a year after 1986	Estimated premium with 100,000 fewer federal government nondefense employees (phased in)	Estimated premium with all three policies	Estimated reduction in earnings premium per lawyer, all three policies ($/year)
1975	0.2298	0.2299	0.2298	0.2277	0.2277	70
1976	0.2779	0.2644	0.2779	0.2737	0.2602	571
1977	0.2874	0.2574	0.2874	0.2812	0.2512	1,373
1978	0.3241	0.2842	0.3241	0.3162	0.2763	1,902
1979	0.2372	0.1998	0.2372	0.2271	0.1897	2,067
1980	0.2973	0.2624	0.2973	0.2852	0.2502	2,193
1981	0.2937	0.2560	0.2937	0.2790	0.2414	2,322
1982	0.2754	0.2277	0.2754	0.2580	0.2103	3,256
1983	0.2873	0.2271	0.2873	0.2679	0.2077	4,565
1984	0.3003	0.2465	0.3003	0.2787	0.2248	4,887
1985	0.3348	0.2508	0.3348	0.3113	0.2273	8,389
1986	0.3398	0.2279	0.3398	0.3133	0.2014	10,194
1987	0.4010	0.2857	0.3751	0.3731	0.2319	13,078
1988	0.3889	0.2810	0.3819	0.3596	0.2448	13,763
1989	0.4100	0.2973	0.3674	0.3783	0.2230	19,878
1990	0.4368	0.3375	0.4078	0.4044	0.2724	17,863
1991	0.4538	0.3622	0.4153	0.4198	0.2897	17,827
1992	0.4870	0.3946	0.4534	0.4522	0.3263	17,456
1993	0.4719	0.3868	0.4400	0.4349	0.3179	18,407
1994	0.4514	0.3706	0.4184	0.4113	0.2977	19,014
1995	0.4295	0.3465	0.4024	0.3865	0.2765	19,312
1996	0.4064	0.3394	0.3714	0.3596	0.2575	17,621
1997	0.3823	0.3260	0.3494	0.3325	0.2434	17,503
1998	0.4527	0.3914	0.3675	0.4013	0.2549	28,380
1999	0.4359	0.3810	0.3495	0.3819	0.2406	27,754
2000	0.4226	0.3675	0.3339	0.3649	0.2212	31,044
2001	0.4451	0.3750	0.3532	0.3861	0.2241	34,461
2002	0.4527	0.3674	0.3667	0.3929	0.2216	35,395
2003	0.4980	0.4123	0.4152	0.4390	0.2706	32,497
2004	0.5034	0.4176	0.4269	0.4427	0.2803	36,706

Source: Authors' calculations.

a. Predictions of lawyers' premiums are based on the earnings premium equation in table 4-1, not on estimates of lawyers' earnings premiums based on the earnings equations reported in table 3-4.

ulating counterfactual scenarios that represent such large departures from observed policies. Nonetheless, a sizable share of the growth in lawyers' earnings premiums would be excised under any reasonable permutation of those policy scenarios. Of course, eliminating entry restrictions would reduce premiums even more.

This analysis should be qualified because there may be many socially beneficial policies, even within our broad categories, that increase the demand for lawyers. At the same time, we did explore the effects of a range of policies on lawyers' earnings premiums, some of which, such as criminal law enforcement and tax reform, have arguably improved social welfare. But we did not find that those policies had a statistically significant effect on lawyers' premiums.

Conclusion

This chapter has provided evidence that the licensing requirement, which limits the supply of lawyers and enables them to organize effectively as an interest group, and government policies, which increase the demand for lawyers as well as the cost of regulation and the liability and patent systems, have had statistically significant positive effects on the growth in lawyers' earnings premiums and that their combination is likely to have had economically significant effects.

The empirical relationships between government actions that affect the supply and demand for lawyers and the growth in lawyers' earnings premiums provide critical additional evidence that we have, in fact, measured the effects of market inefficiencies. For if we have instead measured the returns to unobserved characteristics, such as skills, why would those returns be positively affected by an increase in the number of lawyers? Why would government policies affect the returns to lawyers' skills but have much less effect on the returns to physicians' and dentists' skills? In a nutshell, why would lawyers be the only interest group in the United States that has been unable to significantly benefit from entry restrictions even though, unlike other interest groups, they also benefit from government-induced demand? Those difficult questions do not arise if one interprets our collective findings as evidence that market inefficiencies caused by the regulation of entry into the profession and inefficient policies that increase the demand for lawyers have enabled lawyers to earn large earnings premiums that are widely shared among the profession.

CHAPTER FIVE

Welfare Costs

Theoretical and empirical evidence indicates that entry restrictions created by occupational licensing and the increased demand for legal services caused by certain inefficient government policies have enabled lawyers to earn premiums that result not merely in lump-sum income transfers but also in a substantial deadweight loss to the U.S. economy from inflated prices for legal services. In all likelihood, lawyers' inefficient earnings premiums are shared with law school administrators and faculty because the existence of those premiums enables law schools to sharply raise their tuition to students, who envision large lifetime earnings.[1] Generally, entry barriers capable of generating earnings premiums are also associated with lower service quality; in the case of lawyers, the result may be less innovation in legal services. Finally, the existence of increased earnings in the legal profession may have led to a misallocation of labor by distorting occupational choices and given lawyers an incentive to preserve those earnings by supporting certain inefficient policies and opposing constructive policy reforms. In this chapter, we summarize the costs of lawyers' earnings premiums and document more fully lawyers' behavior as an influential interest group.

1. According to the National Center for Educational Statistics, average law school tuition increased 80 percent in real terms from 1987 to 2001 compared with increases of 42 percent in medical school tuition, 48 percent in pharmacy school tuition, and 55 percent in dental school tuition.

Deadweight Loss, Suboptimal Service, and Distorted Occupational Choices

To the extent that we can interpret the occupational earnings premium to lawyers as capturing a market inefficiency, we can use the standard formula $0.5 \cdot TR \cdot \varepsilon \cdot m^2$ to approximate the welfare cost to society from prices for legal services that are inflated above (constant) marginal cost. In this formula TR is the total amount of annual revenues (spending) for legal services, ε is the elasticity of demand for legal services, and m is the percent markup of the price of legal services above the competitive price. Assuming a demand elasticity for legal services of –0.4 (reported in McConnell and Brue 2004); a markup of 50 percent, which is aligned with the occupational earnings premium for lawyers in the most recent years of our CPS sample; and national spending on lawyers of approximately \$200 billion annually, the formula yields a \$10 billion annual welfare loss. Although we are unable to decompose this cost in terms of the effect of entry regulations and government-induced demand from inefficient policies, both inefficiencies contribute to the loss.[2]

The welfare loss would be greater if it were based on a demand elasticity that exceeds –0.4 (in absolute value) and on our (uncorrected) estimate of earnings premiums using the Panel Study of Income Dynamics, and it would be smaller if it were based on a demand elasticity that is less than –0.4 (in absolute value) and if it accounted for any bias attributable to unobserved skills. In either case, the deadweight loss is likely to be in the billions of dollars.[3]

Regulatory restrictions on the operation of and competition in any market are likely to raise prices, reduce service quality, and impede innovative activity. We are not aware of efforts to estimate the cost of

2. This calculation also abstracts from the shifts in the supply and demand for lawyers caused by government regulations and policies shown in figure 1-1 and simply takes the existing markup and demand elasticity as given.

3. Kleiner (2006) estimates the annual deadweight loss from occupational licensing for all occupations to be roughly \$40 billion. However, he does not base his estimate on specific percentage markups for each occupation. Instead, he uses an average markup across all occupations equal to 12 percent.

suboptimal service quality in the legal profession, but Hadfield (2008b) argues that regulations have curtailed innovations in corporate legal products and services, raising costs and compromising quality. Ribstein (2010) is extremely critical of regulations that prevent innovations by law firms that could ultimately be of considerable "assistance to the middle class," including publication of legal analyses, contracts, software codes, and other law-related materials; legal ideas in products such as tax shelters, takeover defenses, and risk-management tools that accomplish particular business objectives; legal service technologies that can help other lawyers find key documents and cases more easily; and research and development on specific types of business transactions.

The existence of lawyers' earnings premiums has also distorted occupational choices. We are not aware of previous work that has attempted to quantify the costs of this distortion, and we have not attempted to do so here, but there is little doubt that some people who choose to become attorneys might have chosen to work in a different occupation and might possibly have made more economically productive contributions to society in those fields had they not been attracted to the legal profession by the possibility of earning an inflated salary. Anecdotal evidence indicates that some associates who departed their large law firms, either because they were laid off as a result of the financial crisis or because their chances of making partner were slim, decided to leave law to work in the public sector or to pursue a more public-spirited legal practice.[4]

Private Sector Lawyers as an Interest Group Influencing Policy

Our findings show that lawyers' earnings premiums are partly attributable to inefficient government policies that have increased the costs of regulation, tort liability, and the patent system; hence, lawyers have

4. Lisa Faye Petak, "Young Lawyers Turn to Public Service," *New York Times*, August 18, 2010; Ian Graham (2010), *Unbillable Hours: A True Story*, Kaplan Publishing, New York.

strong incentives to support such policies and oppose efficient reforms. Lawyers have become an effective interest group because, as discussed previously, the legal services industry is unrivaled in the extent to which lawyers have infiltrated the ranks of policymakers. That is, the very people who are publicly entrusted to craft and enforce legislation increasingly come from legal backgrounds. Thus, lawyers not only influence the institutions that affect their industry, they have increasingly *become* those institutions.

Lawyers complement their presence in government by lobbying and advising actively and by making substantial campaign contributions. Many large law firms have practice groups committed to lobbying legislatures and agencies on behalf of their clients to influence various regulatory policies, including patent, environmental, financial, and health and safety laws.[5] In addition, many lobbyists in Washington, D.C., are employees of law firm subsidiaries.[6] The American Bar Association spent $1.1 million on lobbying expenditures in 2009 alone, and this effort was surpassed by the $4.7 million spent by the American Association of Justice (AAJ), formerly known as the American Trial Lawyers Association, during that year. Some former lawmakers have moved to law firms to advise corporate clients how to develop business strategy and navigate the federal bureaucracy. They can work behind the scenes and also advise registered lobbyists, especially dur-

5. Robert C. Pozen, "Inventing a Better Patent System," *New York Times*, November 17, 2009, notes that a bill to overhaul the nation's patent law has been circulating in Congress since 2005. But a fierce fight between the high-tech and drug industries on how to measure damages when a company violates a patent applying to one component of a larger product has kept it from reaching a vote. In March 2011 the Senate passed a bill that would grant a patent to the inventor who is "first to file" with the U.S. Patent Office, thus replacing the current "first to invent" system. The House debate on the measure is in its early stages. Some businesses contend that the current system results in too much litigation from individuals who claim they were first to have an idea although they do not have a patent. Small inventors strongly oppose the Senate bill.

6. Chris Mondics, "Law Review: Health-Care Debate Is Good Business for Lobbyists," *Philadelphia Inquirer*, February 9, 2010.

Figure 5-1. *Total Federal Campaign Contributions from Lawyers and Legal PACs*[a]

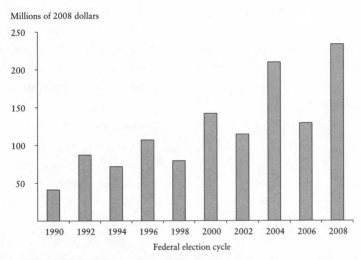

Millions of 2008 dollars

Federal election cycle

Source: OpenSecrets.org and Federal Election Commission.

a. Contributions are the total of all individual and political action committee contributions of $200 or more, and hence are a lower bound on the total amount of campaign money spent by the legal industry. Each federal election cycle lasts two years (that is, the 1990 federal election cycle spans January 1, 1989, to December 31, 1990).

ing the period when they are barred from directly lobbying their former colleagues.[7]

In return for the benefits that they have conferred on the legal profession, the major political parties and individuals running for office at the federal, state, and local level have received significant campaign contributions from lawyers. Those contributions provide access to officials who formulate and implement public policy, signal the preferences of the legal industry, and potentially influence the substance and effects of legislation.

Lawyers have given increasing amounts of money to political campaigns, both as individuals and through coordinated political action committees. Figure 5-1 presents the total campaign contributions (in

7. Danny Yadron, "Lawmakers Move to Law Firms to Advise Corporate Clients," *New York Times*, January 20, 2011. Former House members are barred from lobbying for one year, while former senators are barred from doing so for two years.

constant 2008 dollars) by the legal services industry to candidates running for federal office over the ten electoral cycles between 1990 and 2008. Those political expenditures evidence an unmistakable upward trend over time, even when accounting for inflation—real expenditures have nearly tripled in just twenty years. As expected, contributions are substantially greater in presidential elections than in mid-term elections, but the legal services industry's role as a major contributor has expanded in both types of elections. And while members of other industries certainly make political expenditures, legal services was the largest contributor to federal political campaigns in nine of the ten electoral cycles out of 209 industry categories.[8] The legal services industry also contributed nearly $85 million dollars to candidates running for state legislatures and governorships in 2007 and 2008.[9] In the case of some donors, such as leading plaintiffs' law firms, a larger share of campaign contributions went to candidates who were running for office outside the law firms' home states than went to candidates who were running for office within the firms' home states.[10] The industry's substantial expenditures in the political process suggest that it is well mobilized politically to influence public policies that are in its interests both directly and indirectly, through clients.

It is difficult to provide systematic quantitative evidence of lawyers' influence in generating or maintaining specific inefficient public policies that are solely or partly intended to benefit them, but circumstantial evidence suggests that the profession has had such influence.[11] As a col-

8. This ranking is based on the classification of industries by the nonpartisan Center for Responsive Politics. In the single electoral cycle of the period in which the legal industry was not the largest contributor, it ranked second.

9. This figure, from the National Institute on Money in State Politics, accounts for nearly 3 percent of total contributions to state campaigns, which is an immense share given that lawyers account for less than one-third of 1 percent of the total population.

10. Mark Maremont, Tom McGinty, and Nathan Koppel, "Trial Lawyers Contribute, Shareholder Suits Follow," *Wall Street Journal*, February 3, 2010.

11. By raising this issue, one could argue that we are implying that the causality in our previous analysis runs both ways; that is, lawyers' earnings premiums are influenced by and influence public policies. We are suggesting that lawyers do influence public policies, but the effect is too subtle for us to model

orful example, the noted and outspoken geneticist James Watson revisited the well-known criticism of the Federal Drug Administration—namely, that it unreasonably delays the introduction of potentially effective new drugs—by suggesting that its commissioner, Margaret Hamburg, condones such delays to give "employment to lawyers . . . and that most people in Congress just want to work for lawyers."[12] As another example, President Obama, a trained lawyer and law professor who received strong support from the legal services industry during the 2008 campaign, gained attention in the legal press for indicating a willingness to consider medical malpractice reform to rein in frivolous lawsuits and for mildly criticizing lawyers for helping firms find ways to reduce their tax bills.[13] But his administration has yet to put forth its own proposals on tax and liability reform that vigorously act on those criticisms.[14]

The plaintiffs' bar, the ABA, and the AAJ have not hidden their efforts to benefit the legal profession by influencing specific legislation. In the 1990s several states—encouraged by the plaintiffs' bar—brought suit against the major tobacco companies on the rather doubtful premise that smoking increased the states' expenditures under Medicaid—a federal program. In fact, a large share of Medicaid outlays is devoted to expenses for nursing-home care of the elderly, which are clearly reduced by early mortality caused by smoking. Many states simply hired private plaintiffs' lawyers to pursue those suits rather than using government attorneys for that purpose. A Master Settle-

---

and is certainly not captured by a regression of year-to-year changes in earnings premiums on policy variables. It is more plausible that the existence of lawyers' premiums may affect the evolution of certain policies over time.

12. Allysia Finley, "A Geneticist's Cancer Crusade," *Wall Street Journal*, November 27, 2010.

13. David Ingram, "Obama Gently Knocks Lawyers in State of the Union Address," *National Law Journal*, January 26, 2011.

14. President Obama's fiscal year 2012 budget proposal calls for $250 million in U.S. Justice Department grants to help states rewrite malpractice laws that are consistent with the recommendations made in 2010 by the bipartisan debt reduction commission such as establishing health courts to deal with medical liability cases. The president's proposal does not put a cap on jury awards.

ment Agreement (MSA) was negotiated between the states and the companies in 1998.[15] Under the MSA, the tobacco companies are required to pay the states an estimated $206 billion over twenty-five years, but a large share of those payments will be passed on to smokers through price increases that are the direct result of the MSA. In addition, the MSA requires the industry to reimburse states for attorney fees from a separate fund. Outside counsel hired by the states can go through arbitration that is capped at $500 million a year; hence total legal fees could amount to billions of dollars.

The ABA has repeatedly pushed to make group litigation tax exempt for plaintiffs, potentially generating more business for lawyers. In addition the ABA and the Department of Labor are proposing to join forces to help all employees in a company jointly file class-action complaints against their employer under the 1938 Fair Labor Standards Act. The existing law requires that employees must explicitly "opt in" in any class action against their company. The number of such class action complaints has increased dramatically since the early 1990s and is likely to increase even more if the proposed new ABA–Department of Labor alliance is consummated.[16] Major beneficiaries of this upward trend have been the plaintiffs' lawyers who pursue those class action suits and in many cases appropriate 20 to 30 percent of the revenues obtained through settling those cases (Estreicher and Yost 2007).

Finally, the AAJ has positioned itself as the strongest voice in opposition to liability reform, and it has also been very influential within the Democratic Party through its large and lopsided campaign contributions. The AAJ has not been content to maintain the inefficient status quo in liability policy but has attempted to roll back other medical liability reforms. For example, the AAJ supports the proposed Medical Device Safety Act, which would make producers of FDA-approved medical devices liable for adverse outcomes caused by those devices

15. The MSA is available at www.naag.org/backpages/naag/tobacco/msa/msa-pdf.

16. "1-800-Trial-Bar," *Wall Street Journal*, Review & Outlook, November 27–28, 2010, p. A16.

and would generate more demand for legal services. The AAJ also sought to increase litigation by supporting the Arbitration Fairness Act of 2009 (HR 1020), which would have invalidated pre-dispute arbitration in employment, consumer, and franchise disputes.

Conclusion

The costs of policies that benefit lawyers at the expense of society are not likely to be completely transparent to the public or to many policymakers. The legal profession is widely perceived to be a high-stress, high-pressure occupation composed of well-educated people, so lawyers' high earnings may not attract significant suspicion.

However, lawyers' earnings premiums *are* associated with a large deadweight loss to the economy. In addition, limited innovation in legal services, the distortion in occupational choices, and the legal profession's counterproductive influence, as a powerful interest group, on the efficacy of public policies, while difficult to quantify, likely adds significantly to the welfare cost. Moreover, those costs are growing steadily, making it increasingly important for policymakers to consider policy reforms to address them.

CHAPTER SIX

The Case for Deregulating Entry into the Legal Profession

Competition in legal services is currently restricted in two ways. First, an individual who wishes to practice law must satisfy an occupational licensing requirement. This requirement clearly bars some aspiring attorneys from joining the legal profession because they are unable to gain admission to an accredited law school or pass the state bar examination and deters others who find the out-of-pocket and opportunity costs of a formal legal education to be prohibitively expensive. Second, because legal services can be provided only by law firms that are owned and managed by lawyers, other nonlawyer entrepreneurs are prevented by American Bar Association regulations from entering the market and competing with traditional law firms.

Because inefficient regulatory, patent, and liability policies that increase the demand for lawyers exacerbate the economic costs of entry barriers, one way to reduce those costs would be for policymakers to enact more efficient policies that would also reduce the demand for lawyers. However, experience has shown that government reforms its policies very slowly at best, partly because the very interest groups that benefit from the distortions those policies create are likely to mount strong political opposition to policy reform (Baumgartner and others 2009). We have argued that lawyers have demonstrated their ability as a well-organized interest group simultaneously to limit the size of their membership, to protect and expand their earnings premiums, and to pressure policymakers to institute policies that benefit their members and clients. Indeed, it would be expected that regulatory, patent, and tort attorneys would oppose reforms of their practice areas that could improve overall economic efficiency if it came at the expense of their own livelihoods. The many members of Congress who are themselves lawyers are likely to be sympathetic to such opposition because their training suggests that they and legal practitioners share a common approach to public policy. And even if policymakers reformed certain policies, some costs from entry restrictions would persist.

In the long run, policy reforms that enhance the U.S. economy's efficiency are certainly worth pursuing, but we argue in this chapter that a more immediate and politically feasible approach to reducing the cost of restrictions on competition in legal services is to deregulate entry into the legal profession by allowing any individual or firm to provide legal services without having to satisfy occupational licensing or ABA regulatory requirements. States would be allowed to provide licensing exams, although an individual could fail an exam and still provide legal services, and the ABA (and any other association) would still be able to accredit law schools to certify those individuals who have obtained the requisite qualifications, leaving consumers of legal services to determine the value of such certification. Entry deregulation would generate benefits that greatly exceed any costs and would even help ameliorate problems in legal training and practice that have been acknowledged by the legal profession.

The Quality of Legal Service without Occupational Licensing

The general argument in favor of occupational licensing is that consumers are likely to be harmed by unlicensed practitioners because they are unable or unwilling to judge the competence of individuals who provide an important service. In the case of legal services, it is not clear that occupational licensing has measurably improved service quality because no evidence exists to justify the ABA's initial accreditation policies. Rhode (2004) argues that, in practice, the ABA and state bar associations have provided weak discipline on lawyers' conduct and the quality of legal services, calling into question much of the justification for licensure regimes.[1] From a distributional perspective, Shapiro (1986) argues that occupational licensing tends to benefit more affluent consumers who place a high value on quality, but when sellers' training levels are observable—as they are for legal services—he points out that occupational licensing does not benefit any consumers. It is likely that people who wish to practice law but who are currently prevented from doing so because they have not passed a state bar examination could, in fact, perform certain tasks competently and that any doubts about that claim should be assuaged by the high likelihood that potential clients would be able to assess an attorney's basic quality with reasonable accuracy.

The Quality of Individuals Barred from Practice

An underlying argument supporting occupational licensing in law is that a minimum level of intellectual ability or talent is required to be a competent practitioner; a licensing requirement therefore serves as a screening device to identify and weed out people who do not meet this standard of competence. However, the screening device also serves to prevent laypeople who could compete effectively with licensed lawyers from doing so legally.

Further, some talented people are undoubtedly discouraged from entering the legal profession because they chafe at the expense and opportunity costs of a three-year course of study that can easily exceed $150,000 and are uninterested in working long hours as an associate lawyer in a big firm to recoup those expenses. California allows such individuals (and others) to take its bar exam, and a required first-year competency exam, without having to attend a law school accredited by

1. Kleiner (2006) surveys the evidence on occupational licensing in other occupations, including teachers, dentists, contractors, and electricians, and finds little support for the argument that licensing has a major effect on the quality of service received by consumers.

the American Bar Association or the California Bar Association. Roughly 15 percent of those examinees pass the California bar, compared with 30 percent of the California Bar–accredited alumni. In other states with less permissive bar requirements and limited spaces at law schools, we can safely assume that there are people eager to take bar exams and succeed in the legal profession but who are currently prevented from doing so. Additional groups may be the graduates of online law schools and foreign law schools, none of which is currently accredited.

Taking a different measure of competence as an example, we note that the average LSAT score for people accepted by a law school was 156—as opposed to an average of 146 for rejectees—from 1991 to 2005. According to the Law School Admission Council, those average scores are each about one-half of a standard deviation from the average LSAT score, which was adjusted to 150 during the period. The average score of admitted students or rejected students is not statistically different from the average score of all test takers, nor are the averages statistically different from each other at the usual levels of significance. It is likely, therefore, that some applicants who were not accepted to law school are as intellectually competent as many admitted students.[2]

We recognize that specific legal training may be essential for providing certain legal services and that some unlicensed and untrained lawyers may not be able to perform certain complex legal services adequately, such as complex contracts and appellate litigation. But clients requiring more complex services are more likely to be sophisticated and therefore better able to determine a lawyer's quality without relying solely on an attorney's educational or bar examination

2. It is also possible to reach this conclusion based on applicants' grades in college. According to the Law School Admissions Council, the grade point average of people who were not admitted to any law school was slightly below 3.0 from 1980 to 2000 and is now slightly above it. The grade point average for people who were admitted to law school has risen from 3.25 to 3.34 during roughly the same period. In addition, the share of people with a postgraduate degree who were not admitted to a law school is actually higher than the share of people with a postgraduate degree who were admitted.

history. Thus, given that substantial earnings premiums have been widespread and commonplace in the legal profession for decades, it is likely that eliminating the licensing requirement would allow a greater number of qualified participants to spur competition in the legal services market and reduce legal fees, creating substantial economic welfare gains.

Concerns that such competition would not materialize and that a glut of new lawyers would significantly raise unemployment in the legal services sector appear unwarranted because until the recession that began in late 2007, a very large percentage of recent law school graduates—even from schools that are not ranked in the nation's top 100—were employed as lawyers within nine months of graduation.[3] To be sure, some recent law graduates and even experienced lawyers have become unemployed during the recession; but that is true of workers in all sectors of the U.S. economy. And, as noted, total employment of lawyers has continued to expand since 2007. Because competent people are being excluded from the profession, some attorneys would probably experience temporary adjustment costs from new entry, but the additional competition should not result in high, persistent unemployment in the legal profession.

Assessing a Lawyer's Competence

Given the increasing ease with which information is transferred, we have good reason to believe that potential clients could privately assess—at least qualitatively—an attorney's quality level. Information culled from the Internet (along with other sources) about a lawyer's track record, level of experience, education, and certification status could serve to educate potential customers quickly and efficiently about that lawyer's credibility and competence. As in most other service industries, potential clients would likely be cautious about hiring

3. Employment rates of graduates of law schools before the recession are available at www.ilrg.com/rankings/law/index.php/3/desc/EmployGrad/2007. According to the National Association of Law Placement, almost all of the recent law graduates who were employed were employed as lawyers.

someone to perform legal services who cannot provide assessments based on previous work or evidence of certification.

Even if lawyers had no licensure requirements, certification schemes could be used to help consumers find lawyers with certain desirable or unusual capabilities. For example, the National Board of Legal Specialty Certification provides certification for trial, civil, criminal, family, and Social Security disability lawyers. Of course, individuals claiming particular certification would be subject to general business laws that could result in their being charged with fraud if they were unable to prove certification claims. Over time, consumers would then determine whether one's education, examinations passed, and certification are in fact signals of greater ability and better service, and reward those accomplishments or ignore them accordingly. Moorhead, Paterson, and Sherr (2003) have actually found in England and Wales that nonlawyers provided better legal service in civil matters such as welfare benefits, debt, housing, and employment than solo and small-firm practitioners provided.[4]

Current licensure requirements may create only the *perception* of quality and increase the demand for credentialed lawyers even in situations where the credential does not add social value. This perception of the value of legal credentials is reinforced by the ABA's long-standing aversion to external rankings of law firms.[5] The dissemination of external information about the quality of legal education and services, while beneficial to consumers, may threaten the ABA's monopoly on

4. Tom Jacobs, "Public Defenders as Effective as Private Attorneys," *Miller-McCune*, August 24, 2010, reports that public defenders in Chicago were found to be at least as effective at representing their clients as were private defenders. One explanation was that public defenders were more effective at negotiating favorable plea bargains in a "courtroom workgroup" model of justice, where the public defender, prosecutor, and judge work together to dispose of cases. New entrants to the profession who do not have sterling credentials may nonetheless work effectively in such an environment.

5. Edward A. Adams, "ABA to Study How Law Firms and Schools Are Ranked," *ABA Journal*, February 8, 2010, reports that, despite fierce opposition from its president, Carol Lamm, the ABA has reluctantly agreed to begin an initial study into how external organizations rank law firms and schools.

legal licensure. In the absence of competition in the market for such information, licensure may even create a false sense of security if consumers assume that state bar requirements and licensure mandates ensure a certain level of quality that does not really exist.[6]

Eliminating ABA Entry Regulation Barriers for Firms

Corporations that are not owned and managed by lawyers are currently prohibited by law from providing certain legal services. In addition to the large pool of individuals who could enter the market and provide a range of useful legal services if licensing requirements were lifted, corporations could also enter the newly unfettered legal services market, further increasing competition and lowering prices.

As described in Rebitzer and Taylor (2007), law firms are currently organized as partnerships that employ associates and generally conduct "up-or-out" promotion contests, where a small fraction of associates are invited to become partners. The authors argue that law firms are organized in this fashion because an associate's knowledge of the needs and interests of clients is a key asset. Thus, a law firm protects its assets by offering its best associates a share of its profits in the form of a partnership. Although a law firm incurs the cost of terminating experienced and talented lawyers and hiring new inexperienced lawyers, the up-or-out organizational form maximizes surplus per partner and reduces the incentives of partners to leave and possibly take their clients to another law firm.

An alternative organizational form is a public corporation. But ABA regulations (such as Model Rule 5.4) prohibit firms from selling equity shares in law firms to nonlawyers, which effectively limits sources of financing, professional engagement with nonlawyers, and the range of services that can be offered. The fact that law firms are not pressing for

6. Elizabeth Wurtzel, "Testing, Testing . . . What Exactly Does the Bar Exam Test?" Brennan Center for Justice, New York University School of Law, July 1, 2010, argues that the inefficiency of law and litigation begins with the "complete waste of effort that is its licensing ritual." Wurtzel calls for the bar examination to be eliminated, but she still feels compelled to identify ways that the ABA could keep a lid on the number of lawyers in the profession.

changes to this rule strongly suggests that they are satisfied with its restriction.[7] Partners may benefit from the rule because they are under less pressure to fend off efforts by competitors to attract knowledge-based assets and clients. If this postulate is correct, it is not surprising that large law firms rarely advertise on television or on the Internet.[8]

Ribstein (2008) suggests that the ABA's regulation of law firms has prevented many public and private corporations from competing with private law firms. Some of those firms are well positioned to offer specific types of legal advice—for example, investment banks could offer financial and legal services or large corporations could blend finance, accounting, and legal expertise—which, if they were permitted to do so, would increase efficiency and reduce the overall cost of legal services. Hence, the ABA's restriction on organizational form is likely to be another source of lawyers' earnings premiums and should be eliminated unless there is a compelling reason for prohibiting non-law firms from offering a full range of legal services.[9] The ABA's rationale for its rule is that a law firm must avoid a potential conflict of interest between its loyalty to clients and its loyalty to shareholders, but it is difficult to understand why firms in certain other industries that operate ethically as public corporations would not face similar conflicts.

7. Jacoby and Meyers Law Offices have recently filed lawsuits challenging state laws that prohibit nonattorneys from owning stakes in law firms on the grounds that the restrictions have hurt their ability to raise capital to cover technology and expansion costs.

8. Law firms can advertise on television, although some states prevent endorsements from current clients, require that actors be identified as such, and so on. Some lawyers pay a modest fee or make efforts to be listed in publications that purport to identify the top lawyers by specialty in specific cities and in the country.

9. Ribstein (2009) suggests another reason why ABA regulations should be modified. He argues that the partnership model of large U.S. law firms is failing and that changes in ABA regulations that allow for alternative organizational forms may enhance law firms' financial stability by enabling them to secure outside capital and equity financing.

Benefits to Lawyers from Entry Deregulation

Although entry deregulation would reduce lawyers' earnings, it could benefit lawyers and people who are thinking about becoming a lawyer in other ways. By reducing earnings premiums, deregulating entry into the legal profession would reduce the likelihood that some individuals make a socially and privately suboptimal career choice to become a lawyer in pursuit of high earnings. The ABA has recently become concerned that potential law students lack awareness about the distribution of earnings in the legal profession and is therefore considering measures that would make clear that "astronomical salaries reflect just the top 3 percent of students who go to the top 10 law firms."[10] But ABA actions would not be necessary if competition reduced premiums that contributed to those "astronomical salaries" because potential law students would be much less likely to have misimpressions about their potential earnings following their completion of law school. For those people who choose to become a lawyer, entry deregulation would benefit them at various stages of their career.

Beginning with law school, increases in tuition, which in part reflect the future premiums to be earned by lawyers, are burdening graduates with large debts and inducing them to pursue higher-paying positions at large law firms at the cost of a higher quality of life. According to the *Law School Survey of Student Engagement*, 19 percent of law students surveyed in 2006 expected to owe more than $120,000 at graduation, while roughly 30 percent of law students surveyed in 2009 expected to owe that level of debt at graduation. Allowing free entry of new law schools, including on-line law schools, and eliminating occupational licensing requirements that devalue alternative forms of legal education would put downward pressure on tuition fees.[11] It

10. Debra Cassens Weiss, "ABA Weighs Required Disclosure of Law School Job Stats, More Rigorous Reporting," *ABA Journal*, October 19, 2010.

11. Michael L. Coyne, "Law School for the White and Wealthy," *National Law Journal*, April 11, 2011, claims the ABA's efforts to kill off the Massachusetts School of Law model for legal education were motivated by a desire to ensure high fees for lawyers by charging exorbitant admissions fees to enter its exclusive club. Massachusetts Law School, which has not received ABA

could also shorten the length of the traditional three-year course of study that the ABA requires for a law school to receive accreditation. By eliminating the third year in law school, which arguably does not add much to a law student's preparation for practice, law schools could dramatically reduce the large debt that students incur (Gulati, Sander, and Sockloskie 2001).[12] A step in this direction has already been taken by Northwestern University Law School, which became the first top-tier law school in the country to offer an accelerated JD program that can be completed in five semesters over the course of two calendar years.

Businesses trying to reduce legal costs have become increasingly sensitive about being billed at high hourly rates for the services of new law school graduates who "lack practical training and experience" and who are taught as if they "want to be professors."[13] One general counsel indicated that law schools "cannot continue to churn out people in an academic vein" without realizing that people no longer have the luxury of practicing law for three years to learn how to practice law.[14] Eliminating entry barriers would help bridge the gap between lawyers' training at law school and the skills that are required to produce useful work in practice by enabling vocational law schools and legal programs to become a viable option for training that is attractive—if not customized—to certain employers, beneficial to students who eventually develop a certain type of practice, and possibly influential in the curriculum offered by established law schools.

Hadfield (2010) points out that very few U.S. lawyers actually provide legal aid—free legal assistance to low-income citizens—causing

---

accreditation, currently charges tuition that is about one-third the tuition that ABA-accredited law schools charge. Students who attend the school can take the Massachusetts and Connecticut bar examinations.

12. Gulati, Sander, and Sockloskie report survey results showing that many third-year law students do not attend roughly half of their large classes and that those students who do attend prepare less than half of the time.

13. See, for example, Law Blog, "Who Should Foot the Bill for the 'Worthless' Young Associates?" *Wall Street Journal*, April 13, 2010.

14. "Has Legal Education Gone the Way of the Auto Industry?" *NALP Bulletin*, February 2010.

many Americans in need of such aid to give up in the face of legal difficulties. During the recent recession, legal aid was cut at a time when it was needed to address health care problems, prevent evictions, and protect women from domestic violence.[15] Papers by Sostowski (2001) and Cregler (2002) written in Harvard Law School Professor Jeanne Charn's course, The Legal Profession: Delivery of Legal Services, argue that lower entry barriers could give lower-income citizens greater access to legal services that would be offered free or at more competitive prices. These authors recommend that states modify or eliminate unauthorized practice laws and give consumers the option to employ an independent paralegal or nonlawyer practitioner for many common or routine legal procedures, like the drawing up of divorce papers or the drafting of uncomplicated wills.[16]

Entry deregulation would further address the problem by allowing low-income citizens to choose among a greater number of individuals who would be able to provide helpful legal advice, including people who did not go to law school in addition to well-credentialed lawyers who would be more willing to provide legal aid because they would be able to share responsibilities with certain able people who had been prevented from providing such services. Those expanded opportunities to provide legal aid are likely to enrich some legal practitioners' careers.

Entry deregulation could also help address the "justice gap"— where certain litigants cannot afford a lawyer, do not qualify for legal aid, or are unable to have a lawyer assigned to them because of dwindling public budgets. [17] Free entry would enhance Schulhofer and

15. Karen Sloan, "Perfect Storm Hits Legal Aid," *National Law Journal*, January 3, 2011.

16. Joyce Cohen, "Low-Cost Dental Care Ignites Wide Debate," *New York Times*, November 2, 2010, reports that Alaska has sought to overcome the difficulty it has had in attracting and retaining licensed dentists by allowing certified dental therapists, who receive two years of training but are not dentists, to perform extractions and administer fillings. The American Dental Association went to court five years ago in an unsuccessful attempt to block the program.

17. John T. Broderick Jr. and Ronald M. George, "A Nation of Do-It-Yourself Lawyers," *New York Times*, January 2, 2010.

Friedman's (2010) proposal for a free market in criminal defense services, which would enable indigent defendants to choose their own legal representation. Surely, many of the currently *unrepresented* litigants would be better off, even if they had access only to a capable, albeit uncredentialed, legal advocate.[18]

Finally, a common explanation for the long-acknowledged fact that women partners at law firms earn less on average than their male counterparts is that women partners are less productive than male partners as measured by a firm's revenue per lawyer. Recently, Angel and others (2010) conducted an analysis of the gender gap in law firm partner compensation and found that women are as productive as men. They concluded that the earnings disparity between male and female partners was appropriately attributable to intentional discrimination. Given the controversial nature of empirical studies of economic discrimination—as in our analysis of occupational earnings premiums in which it was difficult to control for all the key influences on individuals' earnings—the authors' study is certainly not the last word on the subject. That said, increasing competition through entry deregulation would potentially reduce any earnings discrimination that exists in the legal profession. For example, corporations that decided to provide legal services would have to hire more lawyers, and many of these corporations would be expected to seek out talented women attorneys who were underpaid partners at law firms.

Conclusion

We have argued that the benefits from deregulating entry into the legal profession far outweigh any costs. By eliminating mandatory occupational licensing of lawyers in the United States and by forcing law

18. Nathan Koppel, "Public Defenders Stretched Thin by State Cuts," *Wall Street Journal*, April 14, 2011, reports that states are struggling to balance their budgets by cutting spending on public defenders, causing some caseloads to climb to more than 450 per lawyer. Public defenders claim that prioritizing legal services within strict guidelines forces them to forgo certain services, such as representing criminal defendants at bail hearings.

firms to compete with suppliers of legal services that utilize alternative organizational forms, we would expect that competition in legal services would sharply increase, resulting in significantly greater variation in the price and quality of those services. Low-cost lawyers and non-lawyers would advertise their services, engage in aggressive price competition, and create a low-cost market centered on offering basic legal services that do not require extensive training to provide. Other lawyers (and law firms) would undoubtedly attempt to differentiate their services as "high quality" and try to maintain high prices, but most of those lawyers and their law firms would be forced to compete more intensely for clients.

On a basic economic level, greater competition among lawyers and law firms would reduce the deadweight loss associated with lawyers' earnings premiums and the misallocation of talented workers who are attracted to the legal profession because of those premiums. This is likely to be true despite the recent recession, which has caused large law firms to lay off associates and nonequity partners, to reduce partners' compensation, and to lose clients who shifted to smaller, less expensive law firms. Greater competition would cause law firms to offer innovative new services and products and would also weaken the political pressure that the legal profession brings to bear on policymakers to support inefficient public policies as the returns from the legal profession's "investments" in political influence diminish because politicians would no longer be able to deliver the premiums they once did. Finally, greater competition in the legal profession would potentially benefit lawyers throughout their careers by reducing law school tuition and the debt incurred from attending law school, aligning law schools' curricula more closely with legal practice, expanding opportunities to provide legal aid, and reducing any wage discrimination toward female partners that may exist.

CHAPTER SEVEN

Toward Policy Reform

We have argued that occupational licensing requirements for attorneys and restrictions on the organizational form of firms that can provide legal services have reduced competition in the legal profession, resulting in large costs and few benefits. Those costs have been expanded by inefficient public policies that have increased the demand for lawyers. Accordingly, we have recommended deregulation of the legal profession to spur competition that would enhance economic efficiency.

From a distributional perspective, concern has developed in the past few decades about growing income inequality in the United States, which has been fueled by strong growth at the upper tail of the income distribution. Kaplan and Rauh (2006) document the legal sector's contribution to this social problem, but their explanations for lawyers' relative wage gains focus on the "winner-take-all" economics of professional superstars. We suggest that the increasing earnings premiums accrued by members of the legal profession may also be an integral part of the income inequality story and that the elimination of entry barriers through deregulation would dramatically reduce those premiums and have favorable distributional consequences.

A fundamental methodological concern that we have discussed throughout this book is that the estimated earnings equations, from which we obtain our estimates of lawyers' premiums, have not controlled for lawyers' unobserved job and personal characteristics that could account for some portion of what we are interpreting as (inefficient) occupational earnings premiums. At the same time, we have presented several arguments and a large variety of evidence that collectively suggest that the level and the substantial growth of the estimated earnings premiums for lawyers over time cannot be largely attributed to those unobserved characteristics.

To summarize, economic theory provides strong *a priori* reasons—constraints on the supply of lawyers and the entry of corporations that could provide legal services combined with government-induced increases in demand—to expect that lawyers may earn premiums that are attributable to market inefficiencies. Second, the empirical estimates of the coefficients of the lawyers' occupational dummies in our earnings equations are consistent with both theoretical expectations and general labor market trends, namely, the slowdown in the growth of the number of lawyers and the growth in regulation and tort and patent litigation during the latter part of our sample. Third, our empirical findings of significant earnings premiums for lawyers are consistent with evidence from legal cases discussed by Barton (2007), who argues that judges favor the interests of lawyers because as members of the legal profession, they share a set of norms, thought patterns, and behavior that result in a common way of looking at the world. Fourth, we have presented formal and informal evidence that indicates that lawyers' job characteristics and unobserved abilities and skills cannot explain our findings of large premiums that have grown over time. Finally, in contrast to our inability to find circumstantial evidence that unobserved variables explain the growth in lawyers' premiums, we have presented evidence that this growth is influenced by variables that reflect important changes in federal policy, but those variables are far less effective in explaining changes in earnings premiums for other professionals such as physicians and dentists.

We should also point out that benefits would still be realized from deregulating legal services even if lawyers do not earn economic premiums. Suppose, for the sake of argument, that lawyers' estimated premiums actually reflect returns to unobserved ability and skills.

Then the distribution of lawyers' earnings suggests that clients discern and pay rates that are aligned with lawyers' abilities. Accordingly, deregulating the legal profession would not reduce premiums, but it would likely benefit clients by enlarging their available choices of the price and quality of legal services without creating additional costs given the capability of clients to accurately discern a broad distribution of lawyers' quality. Of course, we have argued that lawyers' premiums and the price of legal services would fall in a deregulated environment and that a prospective client could rely on various sources of information to assess the quality of legal services.

The benefits from deregulation of the legal profession would also be realized if inefficient policies were not the basis for government-induced demand for lawyers that has increased premiums. Moreover, a deregulated legal profession would not prevent the government from generating socially desirable work for lawyers in the public and private sector. Indeed, deregulation should reduce the cost of such programs.

Our concerns about inefficiencies in the legal profession are shared to some extent by practicing lawyers and government policymakers, but they have yet to call for the sweeping reforms we call for here. The recession that began in late 2007 prompted some responses by law firms to reduce the cost of legal services. Evan R. Chesler, a presiding partner at Cravath, Swaine, and Moore, one of the nation's leading law firms, raised eyebrows by recommending that lawyers stop billing clients by the hour and instead set a fixed price for the requested services to improve the predictability—and apparent reasonableness—of legal expenses.[1]

"Low-cost" legal services firms are starting to appear. Axiom, a law firm with offices in eight major cities, has reduced costs for clients by having limited office space (attorneys work at clients' offices or from home) and by not having partners, but offering median annual salaries to experienced lawyers of slightly more than $200,000.[2]

---

1. Evan R. Chesler, "Kill the Billable Hour," *Forbes*, January 12, 2009.
2. Kashmir Hill and David Lat, "Top Lawyers," *Washingtonian*, December 2009, p. 59.

A number of legal process outsourcing companies have emerged in recent years to enable clients to use the lower-cost services of lawyers abroad to handle the most labor-intensive aspects of U.S. legal matters, especially document review in large-scale litigation. Changes in billing practices and the availability of lower-cost legal services suggest that more sweeping reforms are desirable, especially if those responses fail to gain widespread support as the global economy recovers from the recession. A further concern is that premiums may become bifurcated in a postrecession world, with some lawyers immune from cost-reducing forces and still able to earn large premiums. Indeed, pay disparities currently exist at large law firms as star partners routinely earn eight to ten times the amount that other partners earn.[3]

The federal government's antitrust authorities have not turned a complete blind eye to the possibility that the ABA has taken a series of actions that have enabled lawyers to earn premiums to the detriment of the public. In 1975 the Supreme Court in *Goldfarb* v. *Virginia State Bar* held that a bar association's minimum fee schedule violated the Sherman Act's prohibition of combinations in restraint of trade (Gellhorn 1976). In 1995 the U.S. Department of Justice charged that both the substance and application of the ABA's law school accreditation standards were anticompetitive, but the case ended in a consent decree that merely required the ABA to solicit public comment on its proposed rule changes.[4] Hadfield (2008a) points out that the Federal Trade Commission and the Justice Department objected to the ABA's attempt in 2003 to convince states to invigorate enforcement of unauthorized practice statutes, but the ABA still vigorously supports those statutes.

In a promising development, a few states have actually rebuffed the ABA and have taken very preliminary steps to deregulate entry into legal services. Arizona's legislature has declined to reenact its unauthorized practice statute, and the California bar indicated it would

3. Nathan Koppel and Vanessa O'Connell, "Pay Gap Widens at Big Law Firms as Partners Chase Star Attorneys," *Wall Street Journal*, February 8, 2011.

4. *United States of America* v. *American Bar Association*, 934 F. Supp. 435 (D.D.C. 1996).

not initiate actions under its statute. Such steps suggest a possible path for fundamental policy reform. If some states eliminate the requirement that providers of legal services in their state must obtain a license, and if they express their support for the permission of all types of organizations to offer legal services, then the potential benefits of deregulating entry into the legal services industry would become transparent and eventually spread throughout the nation. In the process, the legal profession would realize additional benefits to the ones we noted because by deregulating all the lawyers we would no longer have to follow Shakespeare's advice to "kill all the lawyers" in order to reduce the cost of legal services and the gross inefficiencies created by the occupational licensure of lawyers and ABA regulations.[5]

5. Shakespeare, *Henry VI* (Part 2), Act IV, Scene 2.

References

Abrams, David S., and Albert H. Yoon. 2007. "The Luck of the Draw: Using Random Case Assignment to Investigate Attorney Ability." *University of Chicago Law Review* 74 (Fall): 1145–77.

Altonji, Joseph G., Todd E. Elder, and Christopher R. Taber. 2005. "Selection on Observed and Unobserved Variables: Assessing the Effectiveness of Catholic Schools." *Journal of Political Economy* 113 (February): 151–84.

Angel, Marina, and others. 2010. "Statistical Evidence on the Gender Gap in Law Firm Partner Compensation." Legal Studies Research Paper 2010-24, Temple University (September).

Auerbach, Jerold S. 1971. "Enmity and Amity Law: Law Teachers and Practitioners, 1900–1922." In *Law in American History*, edited by Donald Fleming and Bernard Bailyn. Boston: Little, Brown, and Co.

Autor, David H., Lawrence F. Katz, and Melissa Kearney. 2005. "Trends in U.S. Wage Inequality: Reassessing the Revisionists." NBER Working Paper, National Bureau of Economic Research, Cambridge, Mass. (September).

Barton, Benjamin H. 2007. "Do Judges Systematically Favor the Interests of the Legal Profession?" Working Paper, University of Tennessee College of Law (October).

Baumgartner, Frank R., and others. 2009. *Lobbying and Policy Change: Who Wins, Who Loses, and Why*. University of Chicago Press.

Becker, Gary S. 1983. "A Theory of Competition among Pressure Groups for Political Influence." *Quarterly Journal of Economics* 98 (August): 371–400.

Bessen, James E., and Michael J. Meurer. 2007. "The Private Costs of Patent Litigation." Law and Economics Working Paper 07-08, Boston University School of Law (March).

Black, Dan, Seth Sanders, and Lowell Taylor. 2003. "Measurement of Higher Education in the Census and Current Population Survey." *Journal of the American Statistical Association* 98 (September): 545–54.

Brickman, Lester. 2004. "Making Lawyers Compete." *Regulation* (Summer): 30–36.

———. Forthcoming. *The Rent Seekers: Lawyers, Torts and Contingency Fees.*

Burkhauser, Richard V., Shuaizhang Feng, and Stephen P. Jenkins. 2007. "Using the P90/P10 Index to Measure U.S. Inequality Trends with Current Population Survey Data: A View from Inside the Census Bureau Vaults." Working Paper, Cornell University (June).

Card, David, and John E. DiNardo. 2002. "Skill-Biased Technological Change and Rising Wage Inequality: Some Problems and Puzzles." *Journal of Labor Economics* 20 (October): 733–83.

Chernozhukov, Victor, and Han Hong. 2002. "Three-Step Censored Quantile Regression and Extramarital Affairs." *Journal of the American Statistical Association* 97 (September): 872–82.

Clark, David S. 2002. "The Organization of Lawyers and Judges." In *International Encyclopedia of Comparative Law,* vol. 16, *Civil Proceedure,* ch. 3. Tubingen and Boston: Mohr Siebeck and Martinus Nijhoff.

Cregler, Joi Pierce. 2002. "The Role of Independent Paralegals in Improving the Quality and Delivery of Legal Services." Harvard Law School, Cambridge, Mass.

Ehrenberg, Ronald G., Marquise McGraw, and Jesenka Mrdjenovic. 2006. "Why Do Field Differentials in Average Faculty Salaries Vary across Universities?" *Economics of Education Review* 25 (May): 241–48.

Estreicher, Samuel, and Kristina Yost. 2007. "Measuring the Value of Class and Collective Action Employment Settlements: A Preliminary Assessment." Law and Economics Working Paper, New York University (December).

Fortin, Nicole M., and Thomas Lemieux. 1997. "Institutional Changes and Rising Wage Inequality: Is There a Linkage?" *Journal of Economic Perspectives* 11 (Spring): 75–96.

Fossum, Donna. 1978. "Law School Accreditation Standards and the Structure of American Legal Education." *American Bar Foundation Research Journal* 3 (Summer): 515–43.

Friedman, Milton. 1962. *Capitalism and Freedom.* University of Chicago Press.

Gellhorn, Walter. 1976. "The Abuse of Occupational Licensing." *University of Chicago Law Review* 44 (Autumn): 6–27.

Gibbons, Robert, and others. "Comparative Advantage, Learning, and Sectoral Wage Determination." *Journal of Labor Economics* 23 (October): 681–723.

Goldberg, John C. P., and Benjamin C. Zipursky. 2010. "The Easy Case for Products Liability Law: A Response to Professors Polinsky and Shavell." *Harvard Law Review* 123 (June): 1919–48.

Gulati, Mitu, Richard Sander, and Robert Sockloskie. 2001. "The Happy Charade: An Empirical Examination of the Third Year of Law School." *Journal of Legal Education* 52 (June): 235–66.

Hadfield, Gillian K. 2008a. "Legal Barriers to Innovation." *Regulation* (Fall): 14–21.

———. 2008b. "Legal Barriers to Innovation: The Growing Economic Cost of Professional Control over Corporate Legal Markets." *Stanford Law Review* 60 (April): 101–46.

———. 2010. "Higher Demand, Lower Supply? A Comparative Assessment of the Legal Landscape for Ordinary Americans." *Fordham Urban Law Journal* 37: 129–56.

Hahn, Robert W., Randall W. Lutter, and W. Kip Viscusi. 2000. *Do Federal Regulations Reduce Mortality?* AEI-Brookings Institution.

Hanushek, Eric A., and Ludger Woessmann. 2007. "The Role of Education Quality in Economic Growth." Policy Research Working Paper 4122, World Bank, Washington (February).

Heinz, John P., and others. 2005. *Urban Lawyers: The New Social Structure of the Bar*. University of Chicago Press.

Henderson, William D. 2006. "An Empirical Study of Single-Tier versus Two-Tier Partnerships in the Am Law 200." *North Carolina Law Review* 84: 1691–750.

Hoffman, Morris B., Paul H. Rubin, and Joanna M. Shepherd. 2005. "An Empirical Study of Public Defender Effectiveness: Self-Selection by the 'Marginally Indigent.'" *Ohio State Journal of Criminal Law* 3: 223–55.

Huber, Peter W., and Robert E. Litan. 1991. *The Liability Maze*. Brookings.

Jaffe, Adam B., and Joshua Lerner. 2004. *Innovation and Its Discontents*. Princeton University Press.

Kaplan, Steven N., and Joshua Rauh. 2006. "Wall Street and Main Street: What Contributes to the Rise in the Highest Incomes?" Working Paper, University of Chicago Graduate School of Business (September).

Katz, Lawrence F., and Kevin M. Murphy. 1992. "Changes in Relative Wages, 1963–1987: Supply and Demand Factors." *Quarterly Journal of Economics* 107 (February): 35–78.

Katz, Lawrence F., and Lawrence H. Summers. 1989. "Industry Rents: Evidence and Implications." *Brookings Papers on Economic Activity: Microeconomics:* 209–90.

Kinoshita, Tomio. 2000. "The Nature and Consequences of Lawyers' Market Regulation in Japan." *Contemporary Economic Policy* 18 (April): 181–93.

Kleiner, Morris M. 2006. *Licensing Occupations: Ensuring Quality or Restricting Competition.* Kalamazoo, Mich.: W. E. Upjohn Institute for Employment Research.

Kleiner, Morris M., and Alan B. Krueger. 2010. "The Prevalence and Effects of Occupational Licensing." *British Journal of Industrial Relations* 48 (December): 676–87.

Koenker, Roger, and Gilbert Bassett. 1978. "Regression Quantiles." *Econometrica* 46 (January): 33–50.

Krafka, Carol, and others. 2002. "Judge and Attorney Experiences, Practices, and Concerns Regarding Expert Testimony in Federal Civil Trials." *Psychology, Public Policy, and Law* 8: 309–32.

Law, Marc T., and Mindy S. Marks. 2009. "Effects of Occupational Licensing Laws on Minorities: Evidence from the Progressive Era." *Journal of Law and Economics* 52 (May): 351–66.

Lawrence, Robert Z., and Matthew J. Slaughter. 1993. "International Trade and American Wages in the 1980s: Giant Sucking Sound or Small Hiccup." *Brookings Papers on Economic Activity: Microeconomics*, 2: 161–226.

Leef, George. 1998. "The Case for a Free Market in Legal Services." *CATO Policy Analysis* 322 (October 9).

Lehmann, Jee-Yeon K. 2010. "Job Assignment and Promotion under Statistical Discrimination: Evidence from the Early Careers of Lawyers." Job market paper, Department of Economics, University of Boston (November).

Lemieux, Thomas. 2006. "Increasing Residual Wage Inequality: Composition Effects, Noisy Data, or Rising Demand for Skill?" *American Economic Review* 96 (June): 161–98.

Litan, Robert E., and Clifford Winston, eds. 1988. *Liability: Perspectives and Policy.* Brookings.

Lueck, Dean, Reed Olsen, and Michael Ransom. 1995. "Market and Regulatory Forces in the Pricing of Legal Services." *Journal of Regulatory Economics* 7 (January): 63–83.

Macchiarola, Frank J., and Michael C. Macchiarola. 2010. "Does U.S. News Make Law Schools More Expensive?" *Minding the Campus* (January 11) (www.mindingthecampus.com).

Malhotra, Neil, Jon A. Krosnick, and Edward Haertel. 2007. "The Psychometric Properties of the GSS Wordsum Vocabulary Test." Working paper, Department of Political Science, University of Pennsylvania (August).

Mandel, Michael J. 1999. "Going for the Gold: Economists as Expert Witnesses." *Journal of Economic Perspectives* 13 (Spring): 113–20.

McConnell, Campbell R., and Stanley L. Brue. 2004. *Microeconomics.* New York: McGraw-Hill.

McKee, Michael, Rudy Santore, and Joel Shelton. 2007. "Contingency Fees, Moral Hazard, and Attorney Rents: A Laboratory Experiment." *Journal of Legal Studies* 36 (June): 253–73.

Moorhead, Richard, Alan Paterson, and Avrom Sherr. 2003. "Contesting Professionalism: Legal Aid and Nonlawyers in England and Wales." *Law and Society Review* 37 (December): 765–808.

Nakazato, Minoru, J. Mark Ramseyer, and Eric B. Rasmusen. 2007. "The Industrial Organization of the Japanese Bar: Levels and Determinants of Attorney Incomes." Harvard Law School Discussion Paper 559, John M. Olin Center for Law, Economics, and Business, Cambridge, Mass. (March).

Pagliero, Mario. 2010. "Licensing Exam Difficulty and Entry Salaries in the U.S. Market for Lawyers." *British Journal of Industrial Relations* 48 (December) 726–39.

Pashigian, B. Peter. 1977. "The Market for Lawyers: The Determinants of the Demand for and Supply of Lawyers." *Journal of Law and Economics* 20 (April): 53–85.

Polinsky, A. Mitchell, and Steven Shavell. 2010a. "The Uneasy Case for Product Liability." *Harvard Law Review* 123 (April): 1437–92.

———. 2010b. "A Skeptical Attitude about Product Liability *Is* Justified: A Reply to Professors Goldberg and Zipursky." *Harvard Law Review* 123 (June): 1949–68.

Powell, James L. 1986. "Censored Regression Quantiles." *Journal of Econometrics* 32 (June): 143–55.

Ramseyer, Mark J. 1986. "Lawyers, Foreign Lawyers, and Lawyer-Substitutes: The Market for Regulation in Japan." *Harvard International Law Journal* 27 (Special Issue): 499–539.

Rebitzer, James B., and Lowell J. Taylor. 1995. "Efficiency and Employment Rents: The Employer-Size Wage Effect in the Job Market for Lawyers." *Journal of Labor Economics* 13 (October): 678–708.

———. 2007. "When Knowledge Is an Asset: Explaining the Organizational Structure of Large Law Firms." *Journal of Labor Economics* 25 (April): 201–29.

Rhode, Deborah L. 2004. *Access to Justice.* Oxford University Press.

Ribstein, Larry E. 2008. "Regulating the Evolving Law Firm." University of Illinois College of Law (April).

———. 2009. "The Death of Big Law." Law and Economics Research Paper LE09-025, University of Illinois College of Law (September).

———. 2010. "The Death of Big Law." *Wisconsin Law Review* 2010 (August): 749–815.

Rosen, Sherwin. 1992. "The Market for Lawyers." *Journal of Law and Economics* 35 (October): 215–46.

Sabot, Richard, and John Wakeman-Lin. 1991. "Grade Inflation and Course Choice." *Journal of Economic Perspectives* 5 (Winter): 159–70.

Sander, Richard H., and E. Douglass Williams. 1989. "Why Are There So Many Lawyers? Perspectives on a Turbulent Market." *Law and Social Inquiry* 14 (Summer): 431–79.

Santore, Rudy, and Alan D. Viard. 2001. "Legal Fee Restrictions, Moral Hazard, and Attorney Rents." *Journal of Law and Economics* 44 (October): 549–72.

Sauder, Michael, and Wendy Espeland. 2007. "Fear of Falling: The Effects of *U.S. News & World Report* Rankings on U.S. Law Schools." Law School Admission Council Research Report Series, Grants Report 07-02, Newtown, Pa. (October).

Schlesinger, Joseph A. 1957. "Lawyers and American Politics: A Clarified View." *Midwest Journal of Political Science* 1 (May): 26–39.

Schulhofer, Stephen J., and David D. Friedman. 2010. "Reforming Indigent Defense: How Free Market Principles Can Help to Fix a Broken System." *CATO Policy Analysis* 666 (September).

Searle Civil Justice Institute. 2009. "State Consumer Protection Acts: An Empirical Investigation of Private Litigation." Preliminary report, George Mason University (December).

Shapiro, Carl. 1986. "Investment, Moral Hazard, and Occupational Licensing." *Review of Economic Studies* 53 (October): 843–62.

Shepard, E. Lee. 191. "Lawyers Look at Themselves: Professional Consciousness and the Virginia Bar, 1770–1850." *American Journal of Legal History* 25 (January) 1–23.

Siegfried, John J., and Wendy A. Stock. 2006. "The Undergraduate Origins of Ph.D. Economists." Department of Economics Working Paper 06-W11, Vanderbilt (May).

Sostowski, Kristen. 2001. "Accessing Justice: Reforming Unauthorized Practice Law, Learning from Advanced Practice Nursing Regulation." Harvard Law School, Cambridge.

Tenn, Steven. 2001. "Three Essays on the Relationship between Migration and Occupational Licensing." Ph.D. dissertation, Department of Economics, University of Chicago.

U.S. Government Accountability Office. 2009. *Higher Education: Issues Related to Law School Cost and Access*, GAO-10-20 (October).

Viscusi, W. Kip. 1991. *Reforming Products Liability*. Harvard University Press.

Warren, Melinda. 2000. "Federal Regulatory Spending Reaches a New Height: An Analysis of the Budget of the United States Government for the Year 2000." Murray Weidenbaum Center of the Economy, Government, and Public Policy, Washington University of St. Louis (July).

Wildavsky, Aaron. 1988. *Searching for Safety*. New Brunswick, N.J.: Transaction Press.

Winston, Clifford. 2006. *Government Failure versus Market Failure: Microeconomics Policy Research and Government Performance*. Washington: AEI-Brookings Institution (www.aei-brookings.org/publications/abstract.php?pid=1117).

Winston, Clifford, and Robert W. Crandall. 1994. "Explaining Regulatory Policy." *Brookings Papers on Economic Activity: Microeconomics* 1994: 1–49.

Index

AAJ (American Association of Justice), 76, 79–81

ABA. *See* American Bar Association (ABA)

Abilities/skills, in earnings estimations, 44–55

Abrams, David S., 44–45

Accreditation standards, law schools, 2–3, 9–11, 98

Altonji, Joseph G., 51, 52, 53

American Association of Justice (AAJ), 76, 79–81

American Bar Association (ABA): accreditation standards, 9–11, 13; antitrust charges, 98; licensing history, 2–3; lobbying activity, 76, 79–80; organizational regulations, 2, 88–89

Angel, Marina, 93

Antitrust authorities, 98

Applicants, law schools, 11–12, 25–26, 45–46, 59

Arbitration Fairness Act, 81

Arizona, deregulation activity, 98

Arnold, Markus, 1

AskMeHelpDesk.com, 1

Austin, Benjamin, 4

Autor, David H., 30

Axiom, 97

Bar examinations: and accreditation standards, 10, 13; legal education requirements, 2, 3; pass rates-salary correlations, 24; in quality argument, 84–85

Barton, Benjamin H., 16, 96

Bessen, James E., 67

Brickman, Lester, 24

Bureau of Economic Analysis (BEA), 19–20

Bureau of Labor Statistics, 18

California, 3, 11, 84–85, 98–99

Campaign contributions, 76, 77–78, 80

Card, David, 47

Certification, 87

Charn, Jeanne, 92

Chesler, Evan R., 97

Clark, David S., 25

Class-action liability suits, 15, 68, 79–80

Commodity Futures Trading Commission, 16

Compensation. *See* Earnings *entries*

Competence measures, 84–88. *See also* Quality arguments

Congress, lawyer component, 4

Consumer protection acts, 15–16

Contingency fees, 24

Corporations, legal services restriction, 2, 3, 88–89
CPS (Current Population Survey), earnings data, 17–20, 28–29
Crandall, Robert W., 61–62, 68
Cravath, Swaine, and Moore, 97
Cregler, Joi Pierce, 92
Current Population Survey (CPS), earnings data, 17–20, 28–29

Deadweight loss, earnings premiums, 74
Demand variables. *See* Earnings premiums, empirical evidence
Dentist earnings, 37*t*, 38–39, 48, 64–65
Deregulation proposal: overview, 83, 93–94; consumer benefits, 5, 8, 91–93, 96–97; lawyer benefits, 90–93; organizational competition, 88–89; and public policies, 97; quality/competence arguments, 84–88
DiNardo, John E., 47
Dodd-Frank Wall Street Reform and Consumer Protection Act, 16

Earnings, as market factor, 16–23
Earnings premiums: overview, 5–8, 55–56; and deregulation proposal, 96–97; and income inequality problem, 95; licensing effects, 57–59; reform pressures, 97–99; welfare costs, 73–75, 81
Earnings premiums, empirical evidence: overview, 55–56, 95–96; distribution patterns, 39–43; estimation results, 32–43; growth patterns, 36–39, 40–41; international comparisons, 25–28; job characteristics effects, 43–44; literature review, 24; methodology overview, 28–32; potential bias evaluation, 50–55; skills/abilities effects, 44–55
Earnings premiums, role of government policies: overview, 57, 71–72; counterfactual scenarios, 67–68, 71; empirical methodology, 59–63; estimation results, 63–65, 69, 70*t*, 71;

interest group influence, 75–81; literature review, 65–67
Economist earnings, 49–50, 65
Elder, Todd E., 51, 52, 53
Employment rates, 86
Entry deregulation. *See* Deregulation proposal
Environmental regulations, 14
Espeland, Wendy, 12

Federal Courts Improvement Act, 67, 69
Federal Drug Administration, 79
Federal Trade Commission, 98
Financial regulation, 16
Florida Supreme Court, 1
Fortin, Nicole M., 47
France, tort system costs, 15
Friedman, David D., 92–93
Friedman, Milton, 3
Furman, Rosemary, 1

GDP share, legal spending, 15, 21–22, 68
Gender disparities, earnings, 93
Gibbons, Robert, 29, 31
Golden Gate University, 10
Goldfarb v. *Virginia State Bar,* 98
Government Accountability Office, U.S., 13
Graham, Bob, 1
Greece, lawyer statistics, 25

Hadfield, Gillian K., 7, 75, 91–92, 98
Hamburg, Margaret, 79
Hanushek, Eric A., 47
Health, Education, and Welfare, U.S. Department of, 3
Health care reform, 16
Heinz, John P., 44
Henderson, William D., 43
House of Representatives, lawyer component, 4

Income. *See* Earnings *entries*
Income inequality problem, 95
Innovation effects, earnings premiums, 73, 74–75

Intellectual property disputes, 14–15, 67, 69
Interest group, lawyer, 4–5, 16, 75–83
International comparisons, earnings premiums, 25–28

Jaffe, Adam B., 14, 62, 67
Japan, 25–28
Jefferson, Thomas, 4
Job characteristics, in earnings estimations, 43–44
Justice, U.S. Department of, 98
Justice gap, 91–93

Kaplan, Steven N., 95
Katz, Lawrence F., 28, 30
Kearney, Melissa, 30
Kinoshita, Tomio, 26–27
Kleiner, Morris M., 36, 38, 50
Krueger, Alan B., 36

Labor distortion, earnings premiums, 73, 75
Law School Admission Council, 11–12
Law School Admissions Test (LSAT), 11, 45, 85
Law schools, 2, 9–14, 25–26, 73, 90–91
Law School Survey of Student Engagement, 90
Lawyers, statistics: bar examinations, 12; law school applicants, 11–12; LSAT test-takers, 11; sector employment, 18, 19*f*; totals, 9, 18, 26*t*
Leef, George, 1
Legal aid, 91–92
Legal spending, GDP share, 15, 21–22, 68
Lemieux, Thomas, 47
Lerner, Joshua, 14, 62, 67
Liability suits, 15, 24, 66–67, 68, 79–80
Licensing requirements. *See* Occupational licensing, overview
Litan, Robert E., 62
Lobby power, lawyers, 75–81
Low-cost firms, 97–98
LSAT (Law School Admissions Test), 11, 45, 85

Macchiarola, Frank J., 13
Macchiarola, Michael C., 13
Mandel, Michael J., 49
Market factors: earnings, 16–23; graphical representation, 5–6; law schools, 9–14; public policies, 14–16
McKee, Michael, 24
Medicaid, 79–80
Medical Device Safety Act, 80–81
Meurer, Michael J., 67
Minorities, occupational licensing, 2
Moorhead, Richard, 87
Murphy, Kevin M., 30

Nakazato, Minoru, 25
National Board of Legal Specialty Certification, 87
Northwestern University Law School, 91

Obama, Barack, 79
Occupational dummies. *See* Earnings premiums, empirical evidence
Occupational licensing, overview: legal profession, 1–3, 9, 82; quality arguments, 2, 83–88; restriction effects, 5–8, 36. *See also specific topics, e.g.,* Earnings *entries;* Market factors
Occupation distortion, earnings premiums, 73, 75
Outsourcing companies, 98

Pagliero, Mario, 24
Panel Study of Income Dynamics (PSID), 50
Partnership structure, justification, 88
Pashigian, B. Peter, 16
Patent system, 14–15, 67, 69
Paterson, Alan, 87
Pharmacist earnings, 48–49
Physician earnings, 37*t*, 38–39, 64–65
Policymakers. *See* Public policies
Polinsky, A. Mitchell, 66–67
PSID (Panel Study of Income Dynamics), 50

Public corporation structure, 88
Public policies: entry deregulation
    effects, 97; lawyer demand effects,
    6–8, 14–16; and lawyer interest
    group, 4–5, 16, 75–83

Quality arguments, occupational licens-
    ing, 2, 73, 74–75, 83–88

Ramseyer, J. Mark, 25, 28
Rasmusen, Eric B., 25
Rauh, Joshua, 95
Rebitzer, James B., 24, 57, 88
Rhode, Deborah L., 84
Ribstein, Larry E., 75, 89
Rosen, Sherwin, 16–17, 30

Salaries. *See* Earnings *entries*
Sander, Richard, 17
Santore, Rudy, 24
Sauder, Michael, 12
Schulhofer, Stephen J., 92–93
Searle Civil Justice Institute, 16
Senate, lawyer component, 4
Shapiro, Carl, 84
Shavell, Steven, 66–67
Shelton, Joel, 24
Shepard, E. Lee, 4
Sherr, Avrom, 87
Siegfried, John J., 49
Skills/abilities, in earnings estimations,
    44–55
Sostowski, Kristen, 92
Specializations, in earnings estimations,
    44
State laws, 3, 11, 15–16, 84–85, 98–99
Stock, Wendy A., 49

Student-faculty ratios, 12–13
Student loans, 90
Summers, Lawrence H., 28, 57
Supply variables. *See* Earnings premi-
    ums, empirical evidence
Supreme Court, U.S., 98

Taber, Christopher R., 51, 52, 53
Tax policies, 80
Taylor, Lowell J., 24, 57, 88
Tenn, Steven, 24
Tobacco suits, 79–80
Tort system costs, GDP share, 15,
    21–22, 68
Towers Perrin, 15
Tuition costs, 12, 13, 84, 90

United Kingdom, 15, 87
U.S. News & World Report, 12–13

Virginia legislature, lawyer component, 4
Virginia State Bar, Goldfarb v., 98
Viscusi, W. Kip, 62

Wales, legal services, 87
Warren, Melinda, 68
Watson, James, 79
Welfare costs, 73–75, 81. *See also* Earn-
    ings *entries*
Whittier College, 10
Williams, E. Douglass, 17
Winston, Clifford, 61–62, 66, 67, 68
Woessmann, Ludger, 47
Wyrick, Justin Anthony, Jr., 1

Yoon, Albert H., 44–45